THE BIG BONKERS BODY BOOK

Written by John Farndon
Illustrated by Alan Rowe

CONTENTS

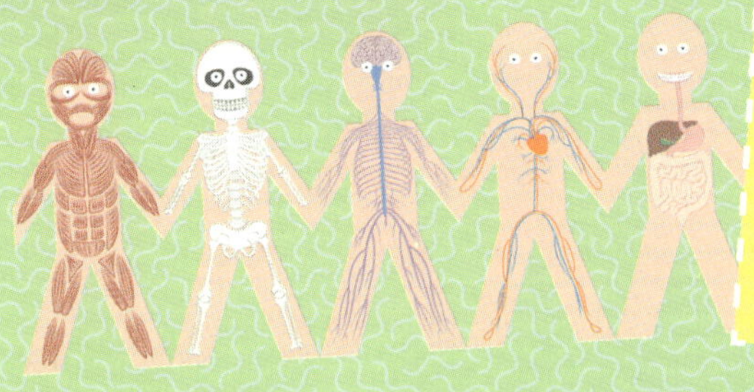

GETTING TO KNOW YOU

MUSCLES AND BONES

ON THE SURFACE

BRAIN, NERVES AND SENSES

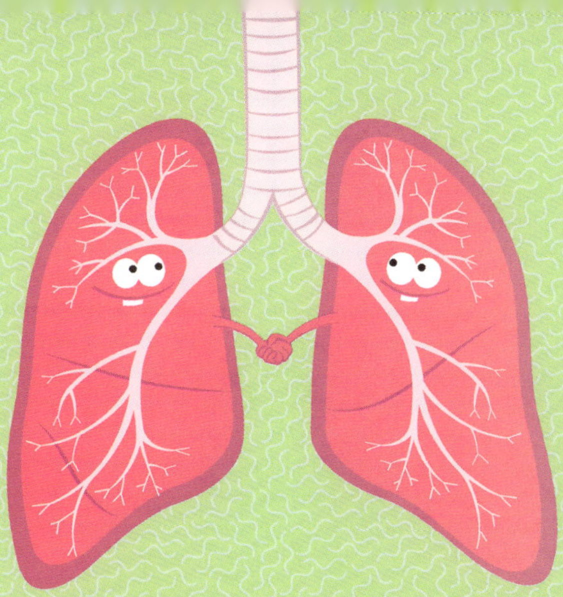

HEARTBEATS, BLOOD AND BREATHING

FOOD, FARTS AND DIGESTION

KEEPING WELL

WHAT DOES YOUR BODY DO?

Your body is an incredible machine that is constantly working away to keep you moving, thinking, breathing and living.

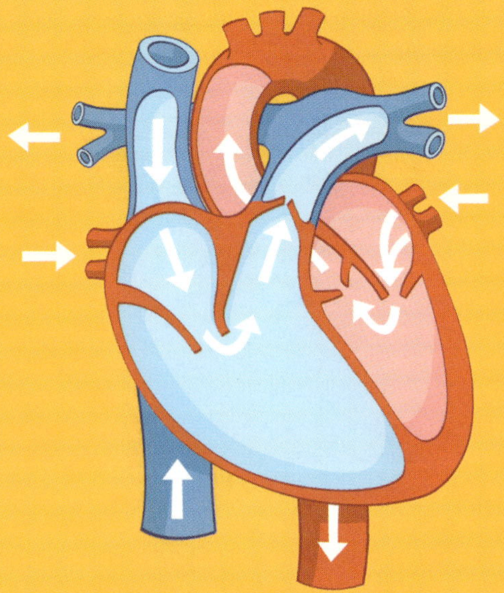

What's under your skin?

Most of your body's machinery is hidden beneath the surface. If you peeled back the layers, you'd find a lot of different parts, including muscles, bones, organs and plenty of icky fluids.

How does your body work?

Your body is all about teamwork. Different parts work together in teams, called systems, to perform different tasks. Here are some important ones:

Muscular system
It makes your body move using muscles.

Nervous system
It sends messages between your brain and the rest of your body.

Digestive system
It is a factory for your food. It starts in your mouth and ends in the toilet!

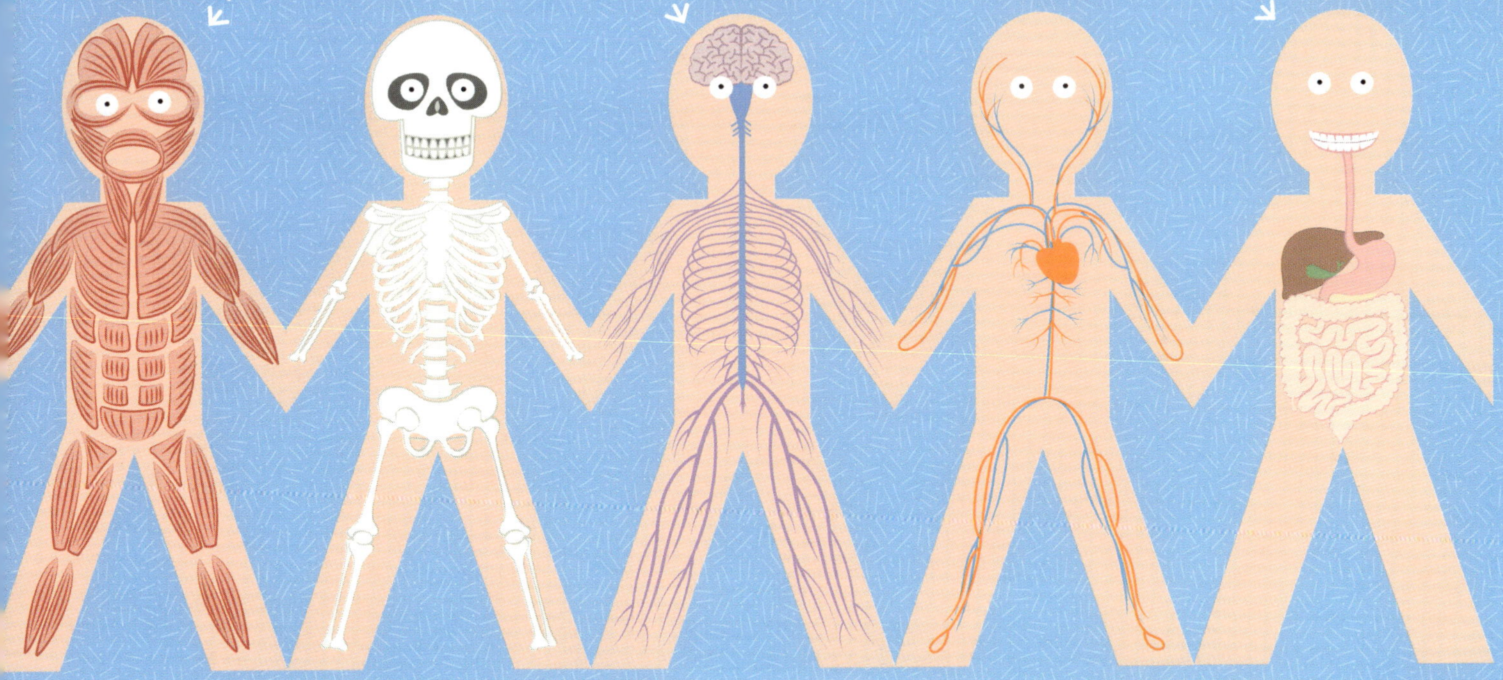

Skeletal system
It holds everything in place.

Circulatory system
It sends blood all around your body.

WHAT ARE YOU MADE OF?

All bodies are made of simple materials. It's how they're put together that makes you so special!

What's your body made of?

Mostly water! But it's all held in place by a crowd of tiny, smart, squishy packages called cells. There are more than 37 trillion of them! Here are some different kinds:

Red blood cell

Muscle cell

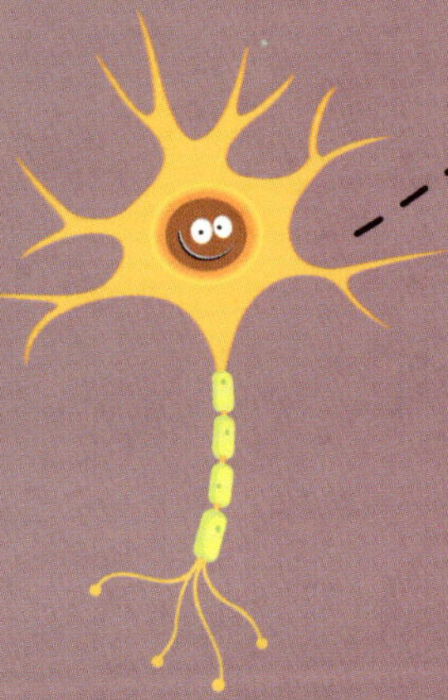

Nerve cell (neuron)

Fat cell

Liver cell

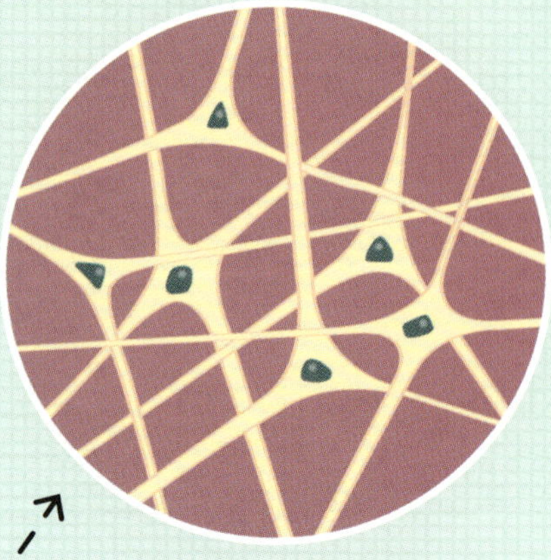

Nervous tissue

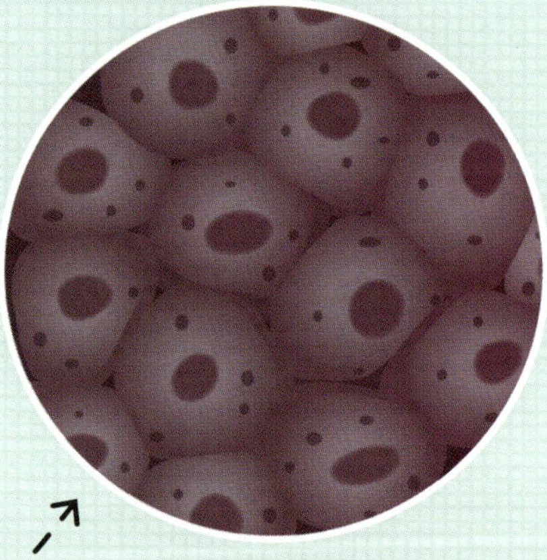

Liver tissue

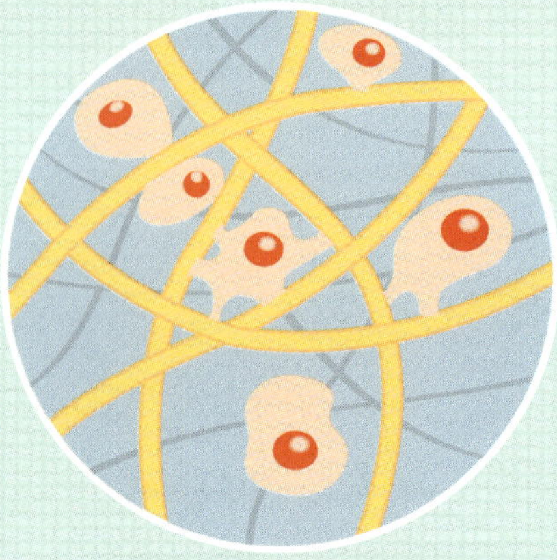

Connective tissue

How does it all fit together?

Similar cells grow together to make tissues, such as muscles, bones and skin. Connective tissue connects different parts of the body together. The spaces between are usually filled with liquid.

What are organs?

Organs are special parts of your body with their own tasks, such as your eyes, heart, lungs, liver and stomach.

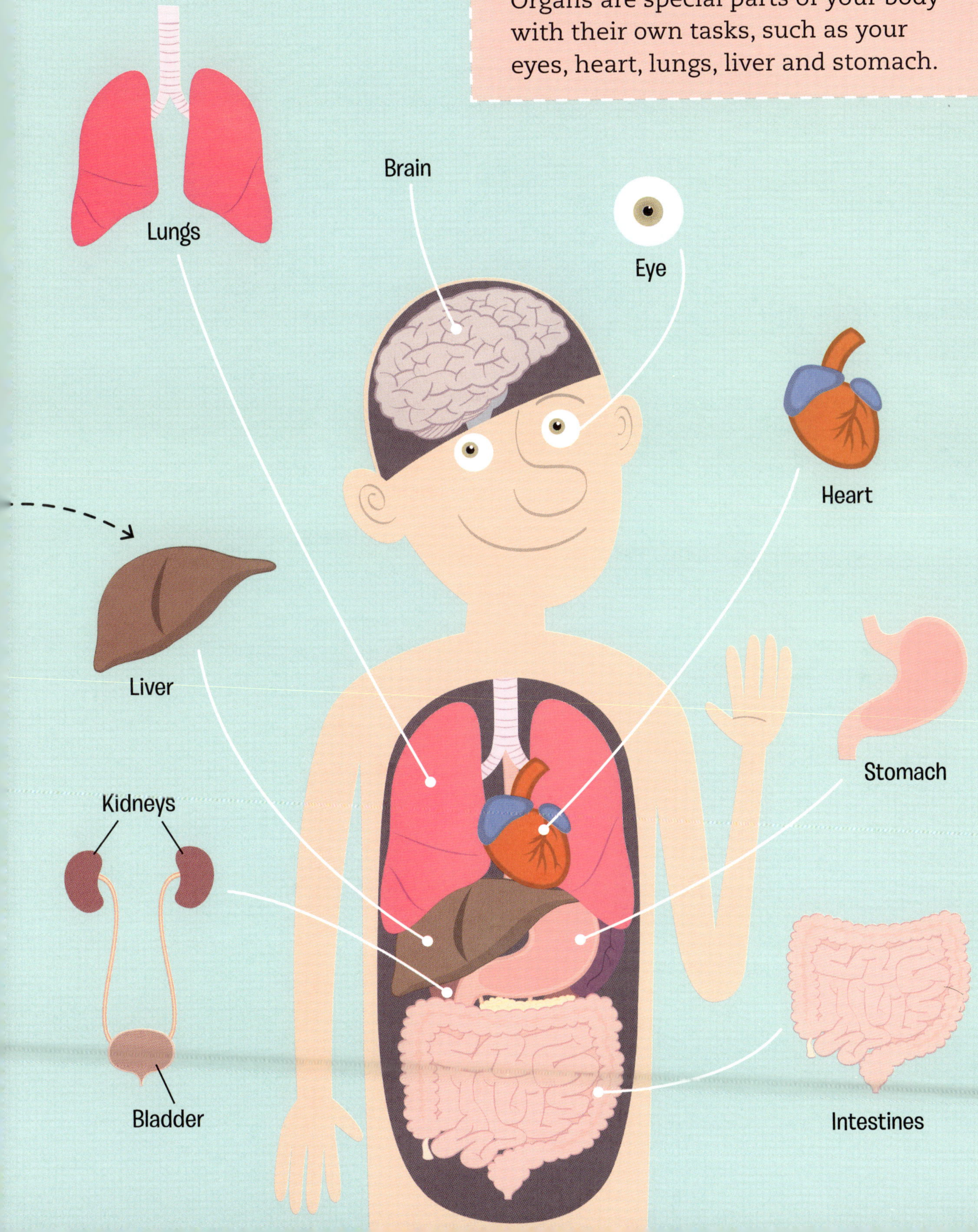

MIGHTY MUSCLES

If you just turned the page, your muscles helped you do it. But how?

What are muscles?

Muscles are bundles of rope-like tissue. They do just one simple thing, get shorter!

Where have you got muscles?

You've got more than 650 muscles all over your body. Here are a few of them:

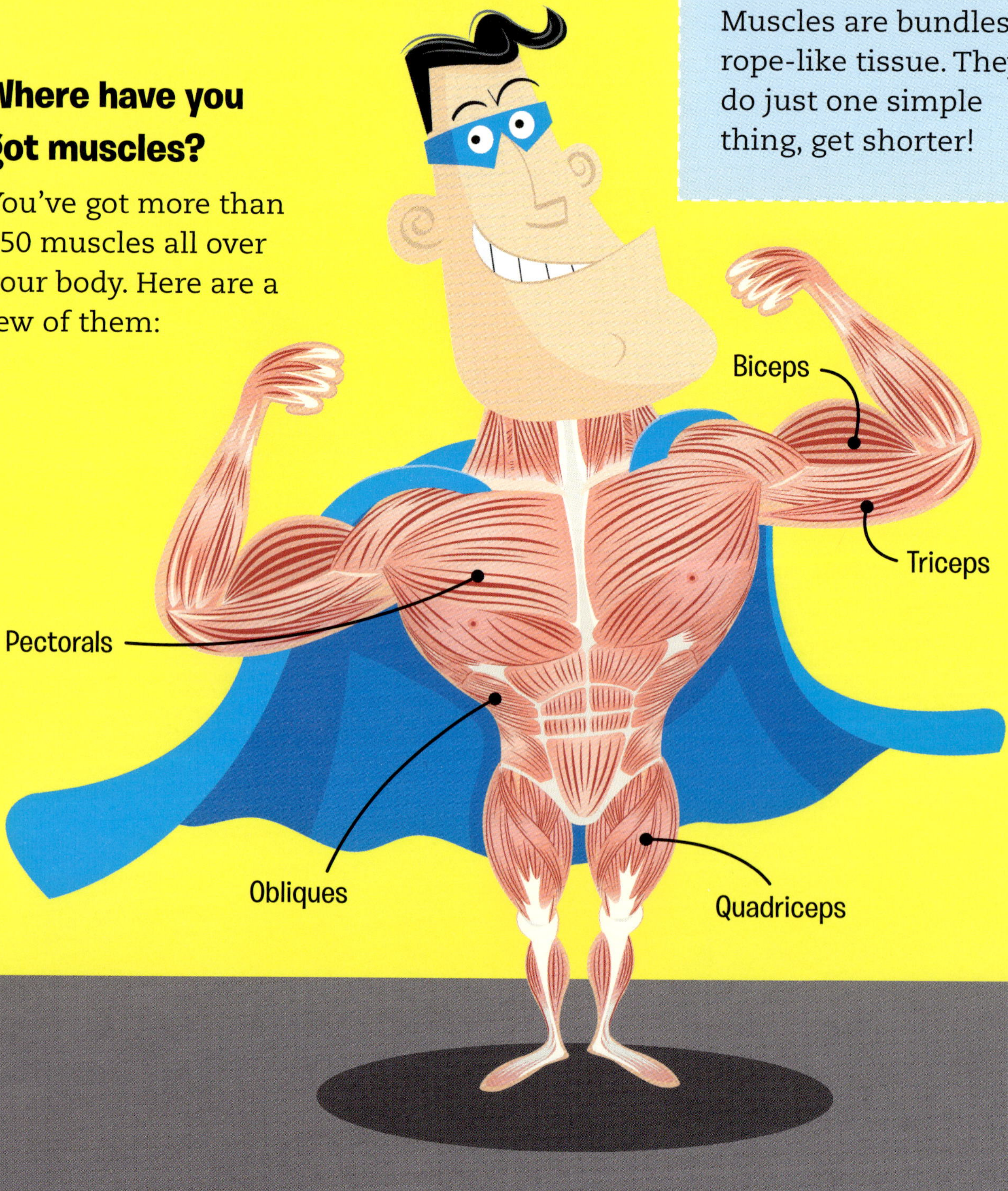

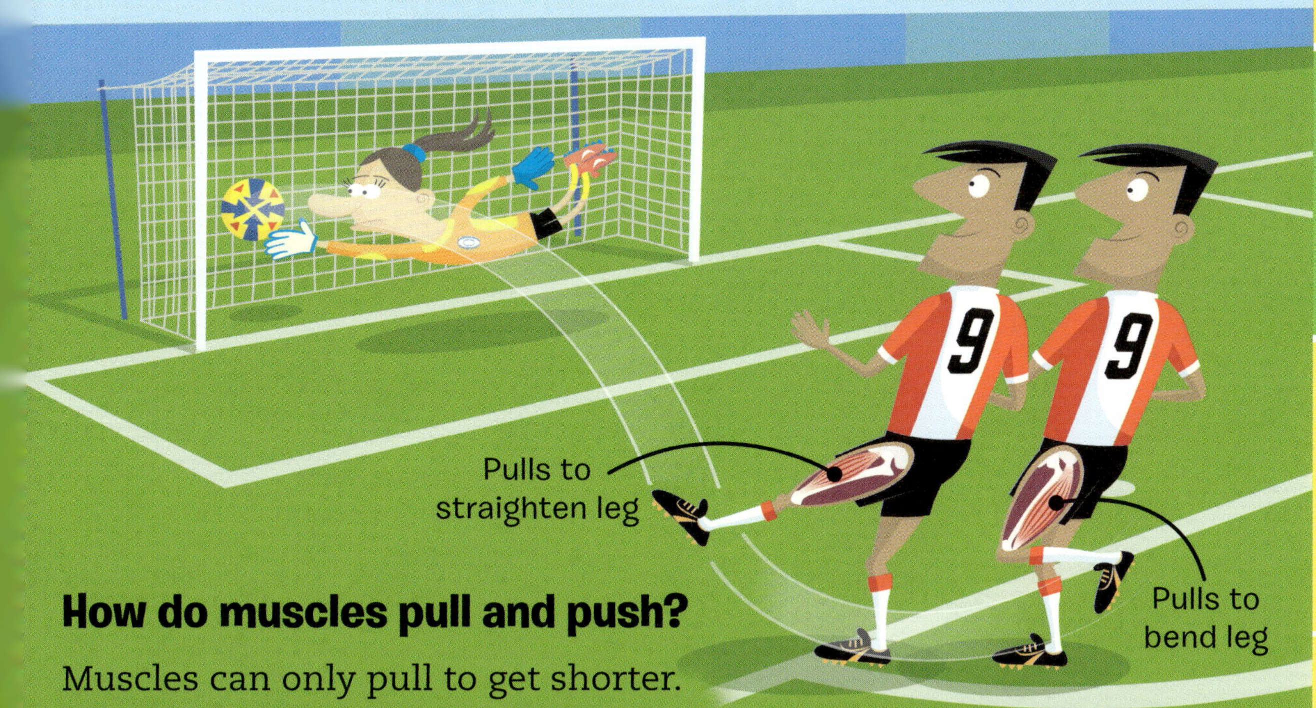

How do muscles pull and push?

Muscles can only pull to get shorter. That's why they come in pairs: one to pull (called the flexor) and the other to pull it back (the extensor).

Biceps

The biceps muscle in your upper arm lifts your hand.

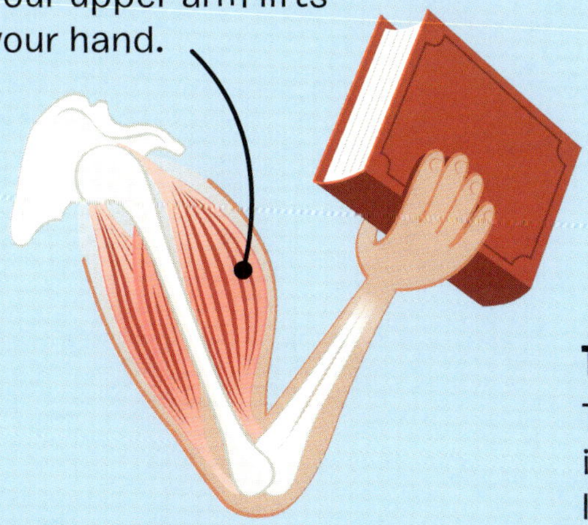

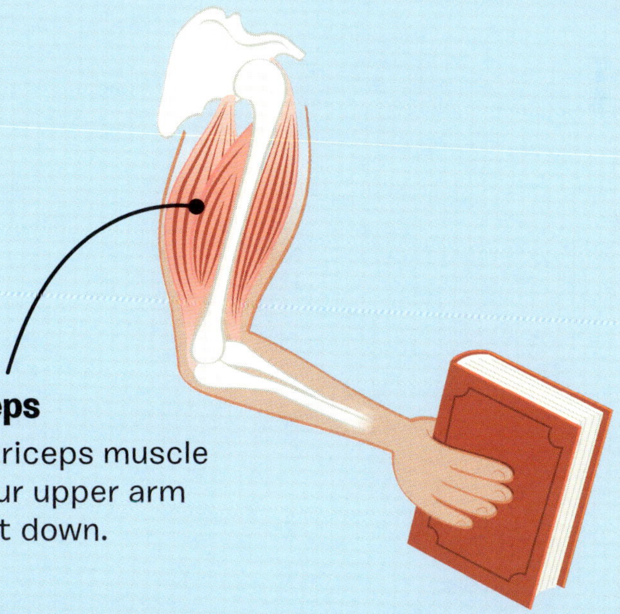

Triceps

The triceps muscle in your upper arm lets it down.

How do you move your hand?

When you picked up this book, your brain told the right muscles to pull, and your hand moved. Amazing!

BUILDING STRENGTH

Your muscles make you strong. Without them, you couldn't lift, pull or push things.

Why do athletes need to train?

Training makes your muscles grow bigger and stronger so they can pull better. If you don't use them regularly, they get smaller and weaker.

How do muscles grow bigger?

When you exercise a lot, the muscle tissue you use starts to get longer and stronger. Then you start to grow more of it.

What's your strongest muscle?

Ever bitten your tongue? Then you'll know! Your strongest muscle is the masseter muscle, which makes your teeth bite together.

(Don't try this at home!)

What's your biggest muscle?

You're sitting on it. Scientists call it the gluteus maximus, but it's really just your butt!

YOUR BONY FRAME

Flesh and muscles are pretty soft and full of water. So what keeps you upright?

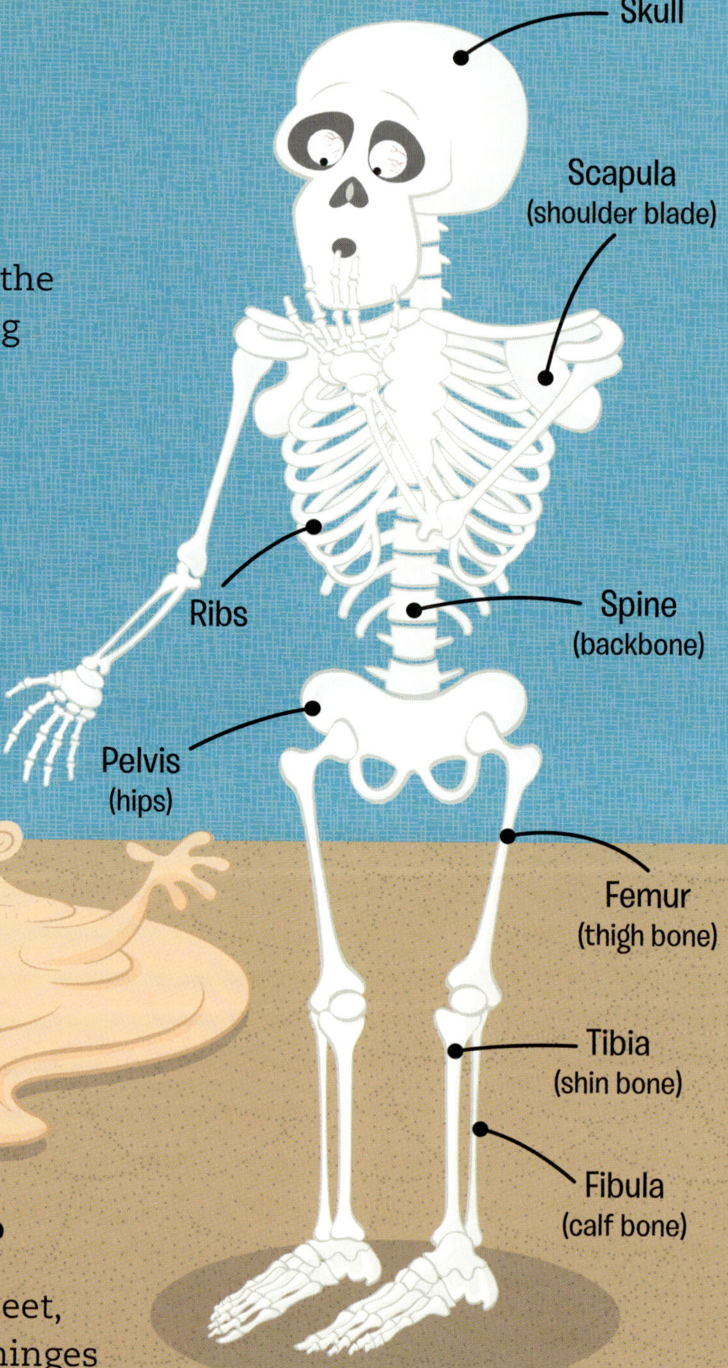

What's your skeleton?

It's a frame of strong bones that all the flesh and muscles of your body hang from. Without it you'd slump like a floppy mess on the floor.

Your skeleton has more than 200 bones!

How does your skeleton bend?

Bones can't bend, but where they meet, they are joined together by special hinges called joints. Most joints, such as your elbows and knees, can bend only one way.

What's your bendiest joint?

In your shoulder joints and hip joints, the arm bones and leg bones end in a ball that sits in a cup. The ball can move in a lot of different directions.

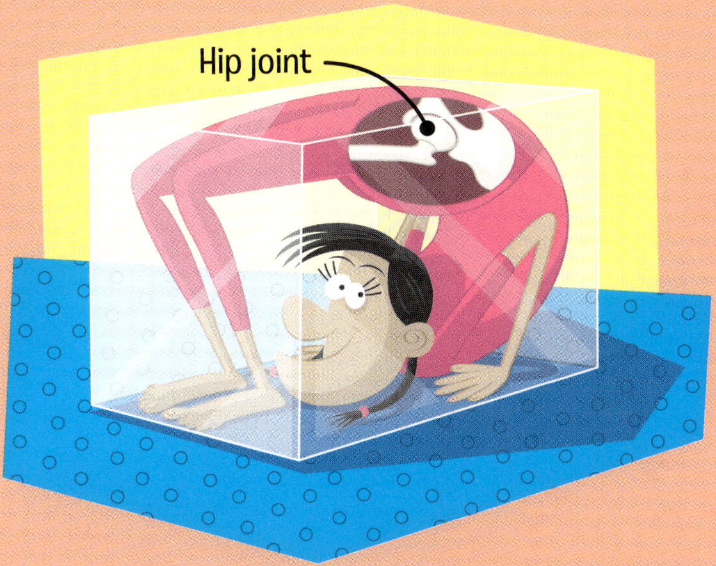

What's inside your bones?

The outside of a bone is solid, but inside it is full of holes like a sponge.

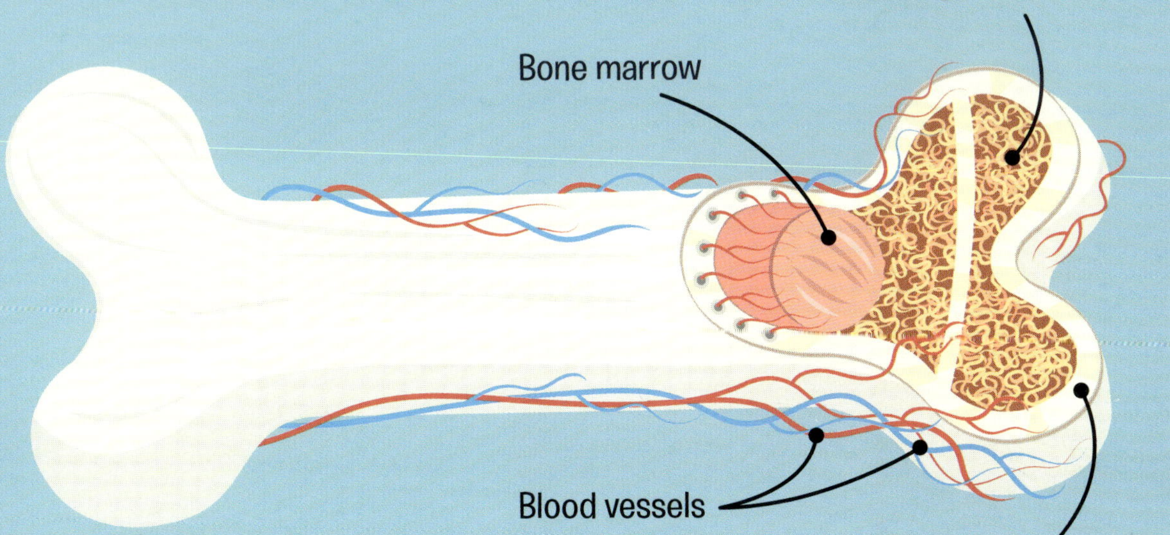

Many of your bones are filled with soft, gel-like stuff, called marrow. Some is red and bloody, and some is yellow and fatty. Red marrow is your body's factory for making red blood cells.

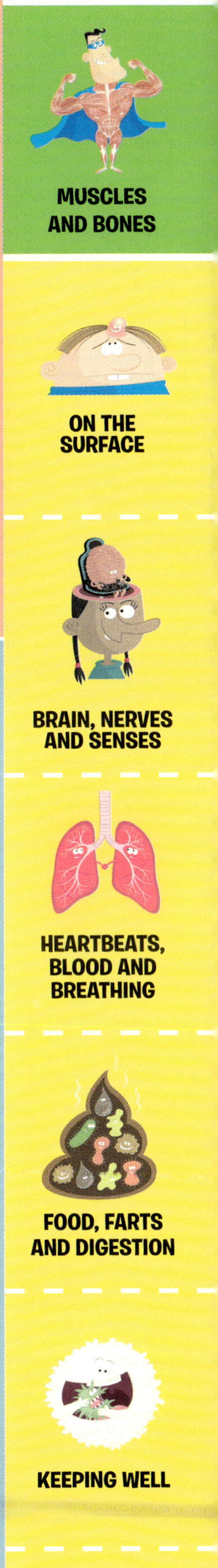

JOINING TOGETHER

Your bones come in a lot of shapes and sizes, and fit together in different ways. It's like a puzzle!

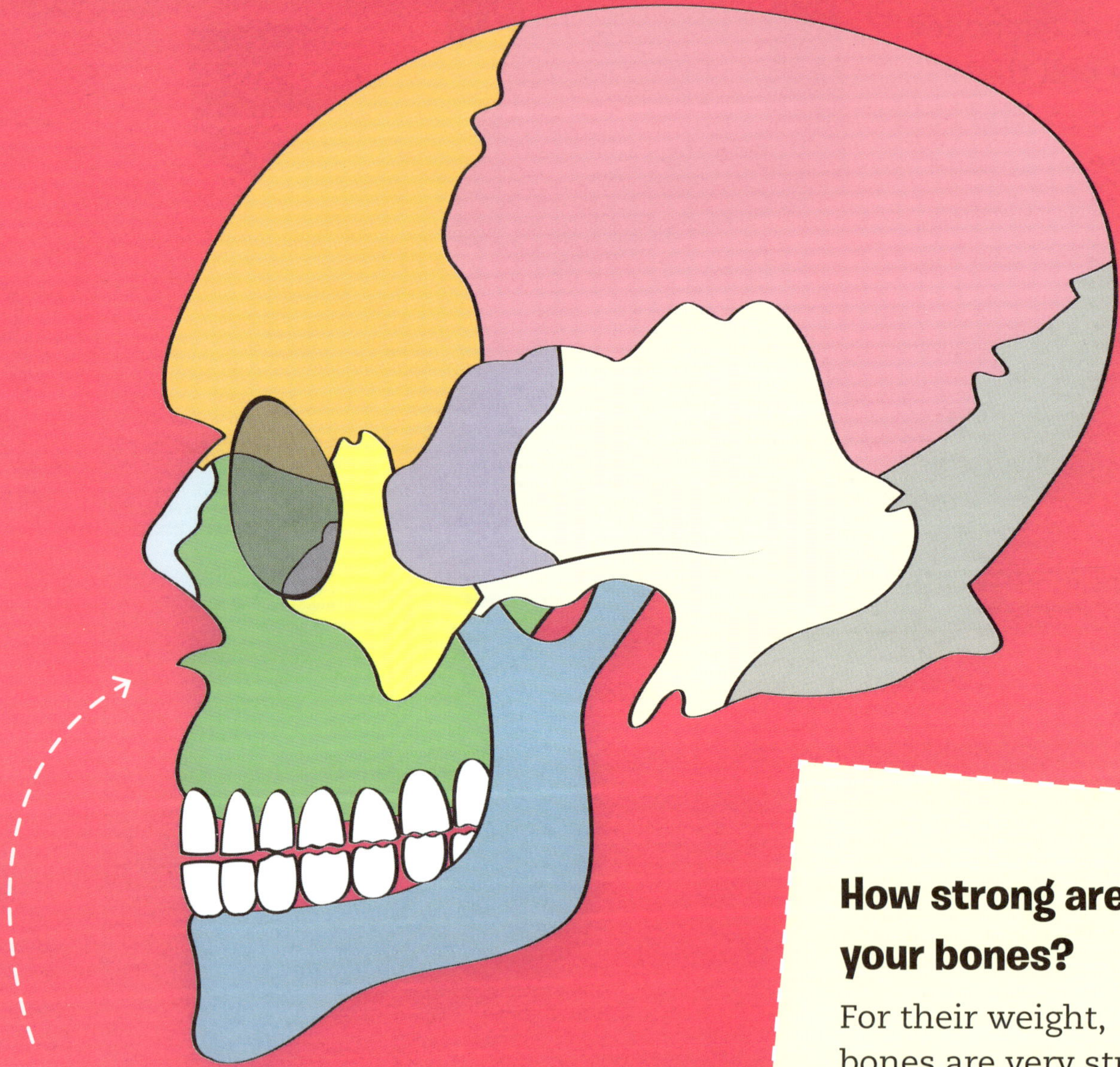

How strong are your bones?

For their weight, bones are very strong. They are four times as strong as concrete! They are also very light, because of all the holes inside.

Why is your head hard?

Your precious brain is protected by a hard case of bone called your skull. It is made from 22 pieces, which are all joined firmly together.

How is your hand so bendy?

It's because each hand is made of 27 little bones, letting it move in many ways.

Your feet also have 26 bones each. So more than half of all your bones are in your hands and feet!

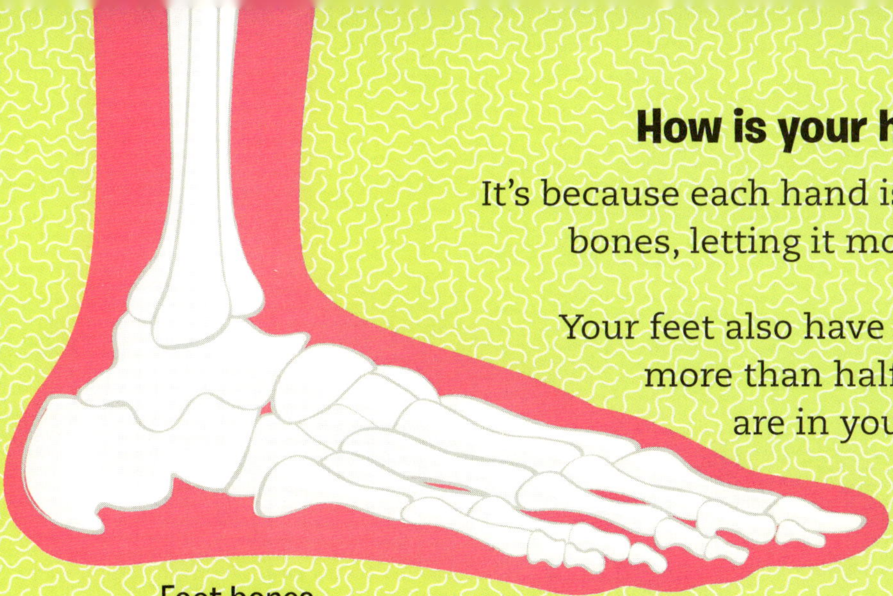

Foot bones

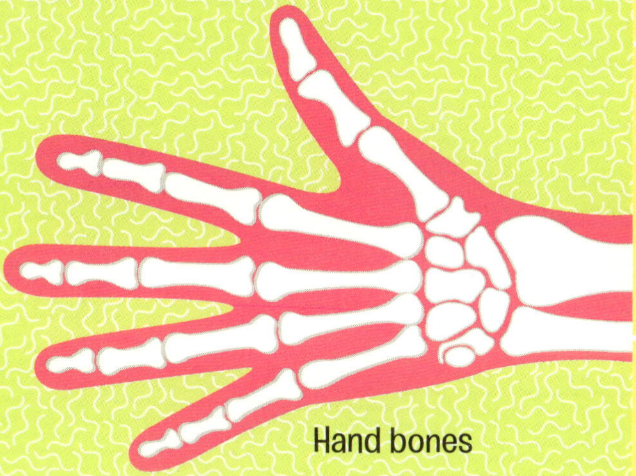

Hand bones

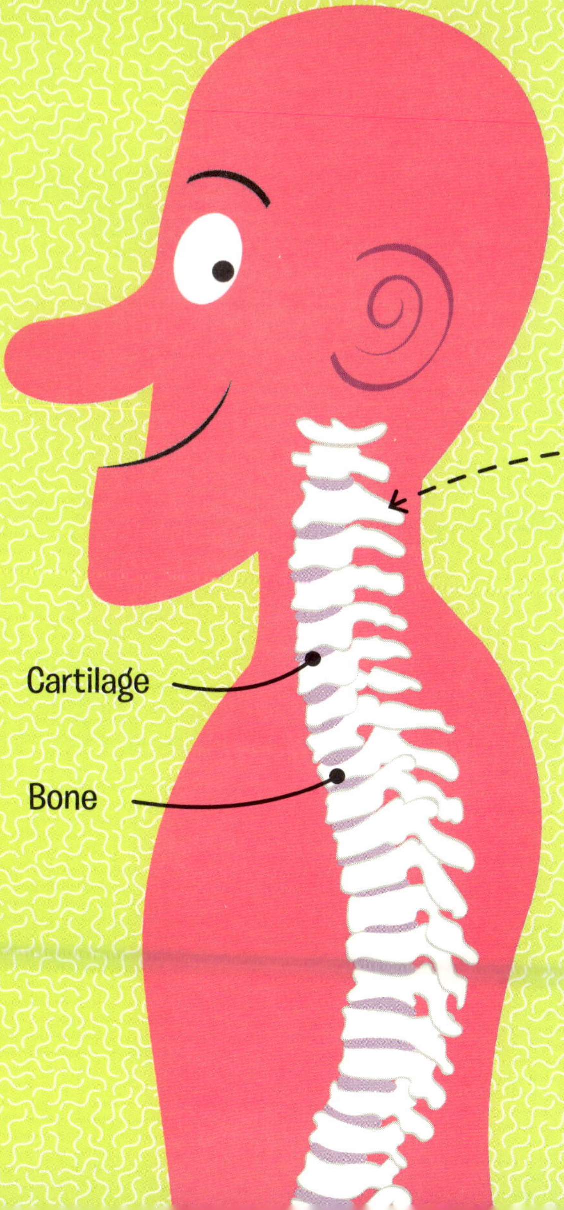

What's your backbone?

It's not just a single bone but a stack of 33 bones. Between each of them is a squishy material, called **cartilage**. It acts as a cushion and lets you bend your back.

SKIN DEEP

Your body is covered in skin, from head to toe. How much do you know about it?

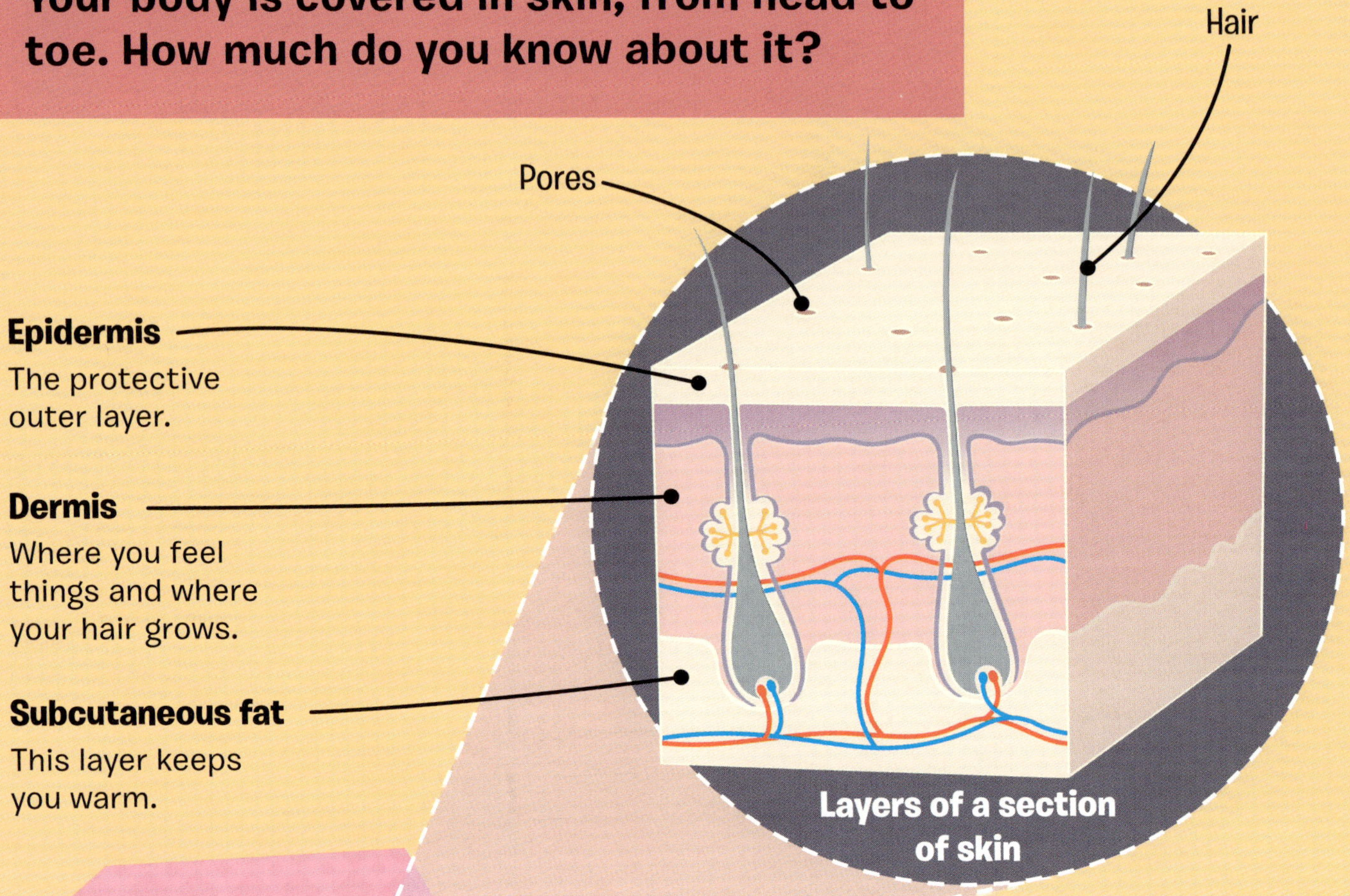

Layers of a section of skin

Why do we have skin?

It's your protective suit. It's waterproof, keeps you warm and it's good at keeping out **germs** and dirt (most of the time).

How big is your skin?

Your skin is the heaviest part of your body and weighs 5 to 10 pounds (2–4.5 kg), about the same as a cat. If you rolled it out, it would cover your whole bed.

Does your skin ever change?

Your body keeps your skin fresh by adding new cells and shedding old ones. In fact, you replace your whole skin every month. You could lose more than 1,000 skins in your lifetime!

What happens to old skin?

You lose more than 30,000 skin cells every minute. More than half the dust in your house is your old skin!

Tiny creatures called dust mites chomp on it all the time. Eugghh!

SWEATY, OILY SKIN

If your skin gets renewed all the time, shouldn't it stay clean by itself?

Why do you need to bathe?

The sweat, oil and dead cells made by your skin are a lovely home for germs!* If you don't wash regularly, you may start to get smelly. Germs can also get in through cuts and make you ill.

*Find out more about germs on pages 68–73.

How do you sweat, and why?

Your skin is covered in tiny holes, called pores. One kind oozes oil, called sebum, to keep your skin flexible. The other oozes water (or sweat), which helps your body keep cool.

What's dandruff?

Dandruff is when a lot of little flakes, made of dead skin cells and oil, form on your **scalp**. It can be embarrassing and itchy, but it's very common and easy to treat.

What are zits?

Zits, spots, pimples (whatever you call them), can form when pores get clogged up with dead skin cells, oil and germs.

Some zits turn red and fill with **pus**. It might be tempting to pop them, but don't! It can make things worse.

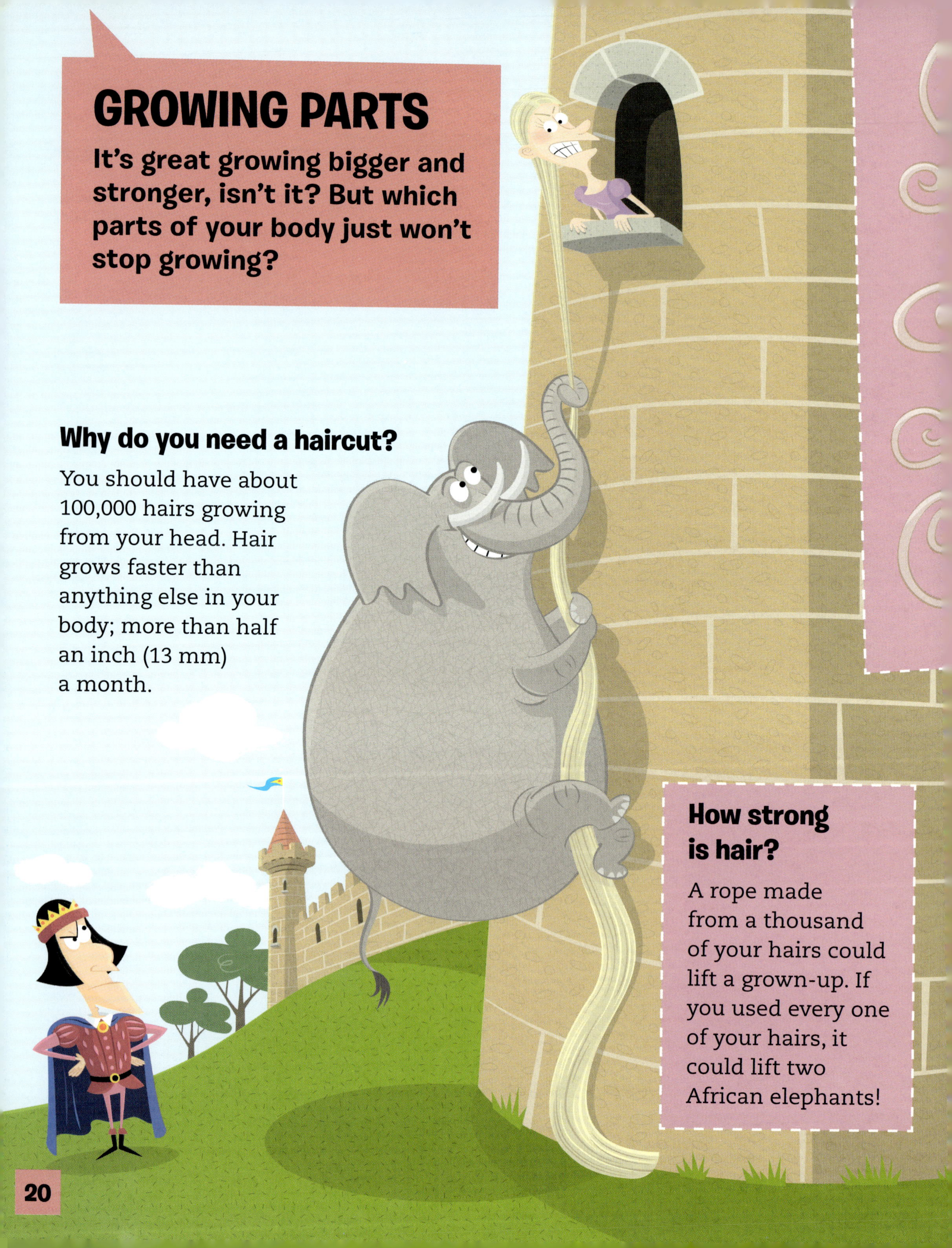

GROWING PARTS

It's great growing bigger and stronger, isn't it? But which parts of your body just won't stop growing?

Why do you need a haircut?

You should have about 100,000 hairs growing from your head. Hair grows faster than anything else in your body; more than half an inch (13 mm) a month.

How strong is hair?

A rope made from a thousand of your hairs could lift a grown-up. If you used every one of your hairs, it could lift two African elephants!

How fast do nails grow?

Fingernails grow faster than toenails, and your middle one grows fastest of all. Your fingernails would grow almost 100 feet (30 m) long in your lifetime, if you didn't cut them.

Why doesn't cutting nails and hair hurt?

Because they are not alive! They are made of keratin, a material left by dead cells. Only the root is alive and has nerves attached (see page 30), which makes it able to feel.

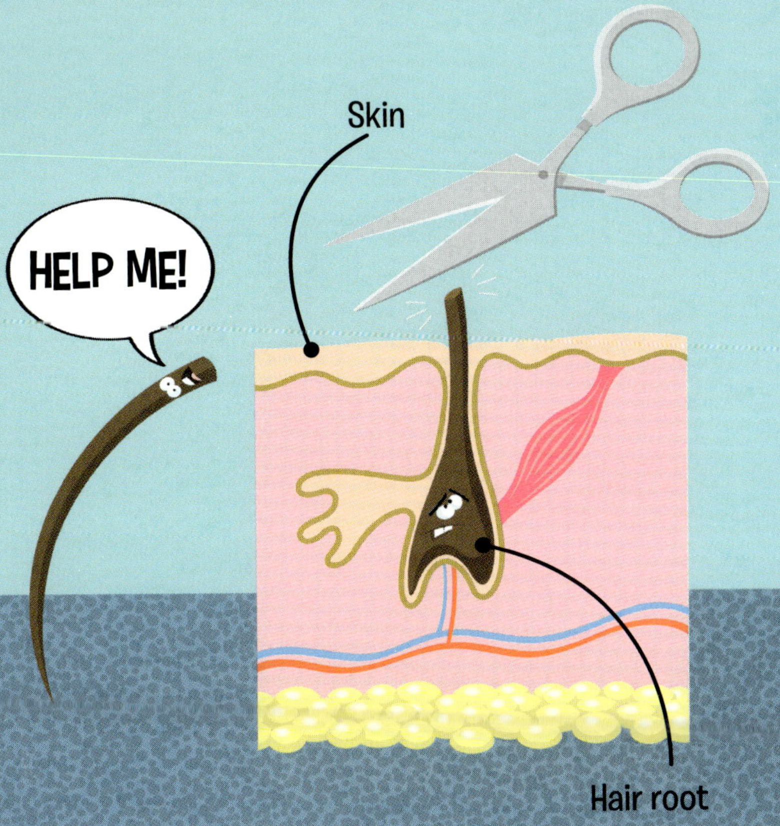

CUTS AND BRUISES

It's your skin that takes the damage if you fall or cut yourself. Ouch!

What's a bruise?

If you fall and get a bruise, your skin is bleeding on the inside.

What's a graze?

A graze is when you scrape the surface of the skin. It can be very sore but doesn't break through the skin.

What's a cut?

A cut is when something slices right into the skin.

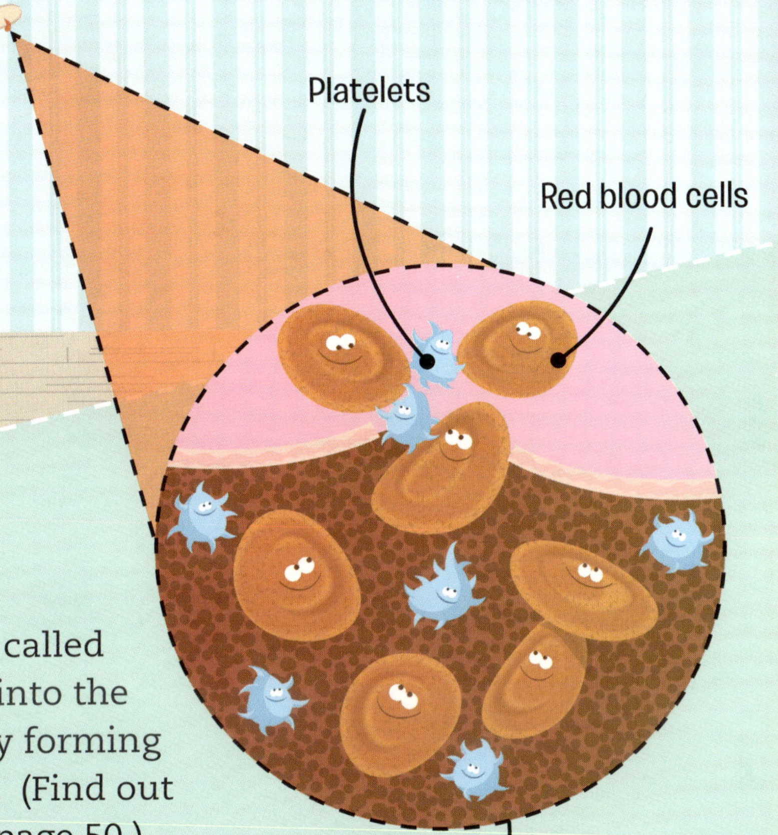

Why do cuts bleed?

Special cells in your blood, called platelets, cram blood cells into the cut. These block the hole by forming a sticky mess, called a clot. (Find out more about your blood on page 50.)

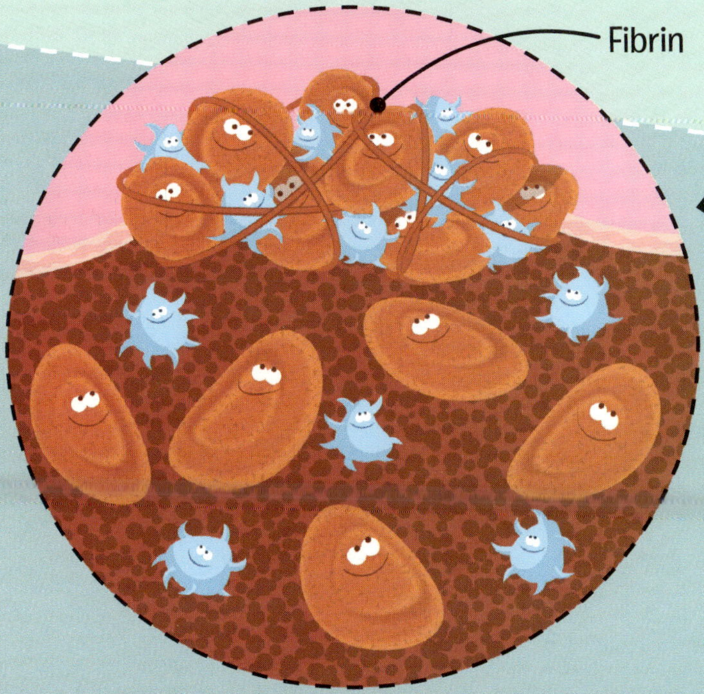

What's a scab?

Within seconds, the clot starts to dry out. Little stringy parts, called fibrin, bind it together to make a scab. Scabs protect your skin while it repairs itself.

DO YOU MIND?

Inside your head is a supercomputer. It's called a brain, and it's always telling the rest of your body what to do.

What does your brain look like?

It looks like a big, squishy, wrinkled walnut. It's mostly made of fat and water. While not the prettiest organ, it is definitely the smartest!

How does it work?

Your brain is like a big messy bundle of wires. These wires are called brain cells, and you have 100 million of them!

They constantly zap messages to each other, making trillions of connections!

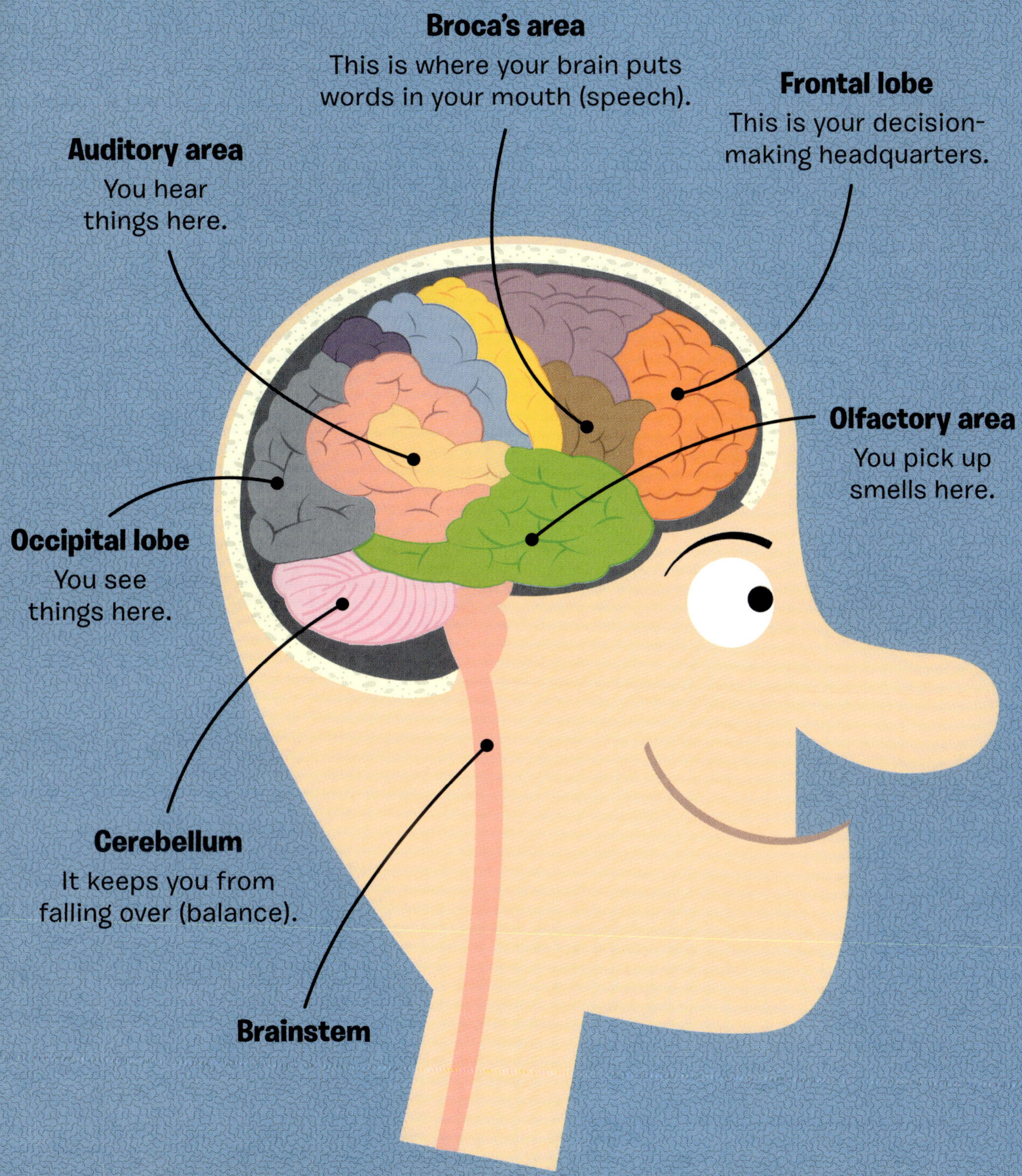

What goes on where?

Each part of your brain has its own job controlling what you do, from speaking to moving.

YOU'VE GOT A NERVE!

Our body has its own messaging system called nerves. They send information from every part of your body, and keep it all under control.

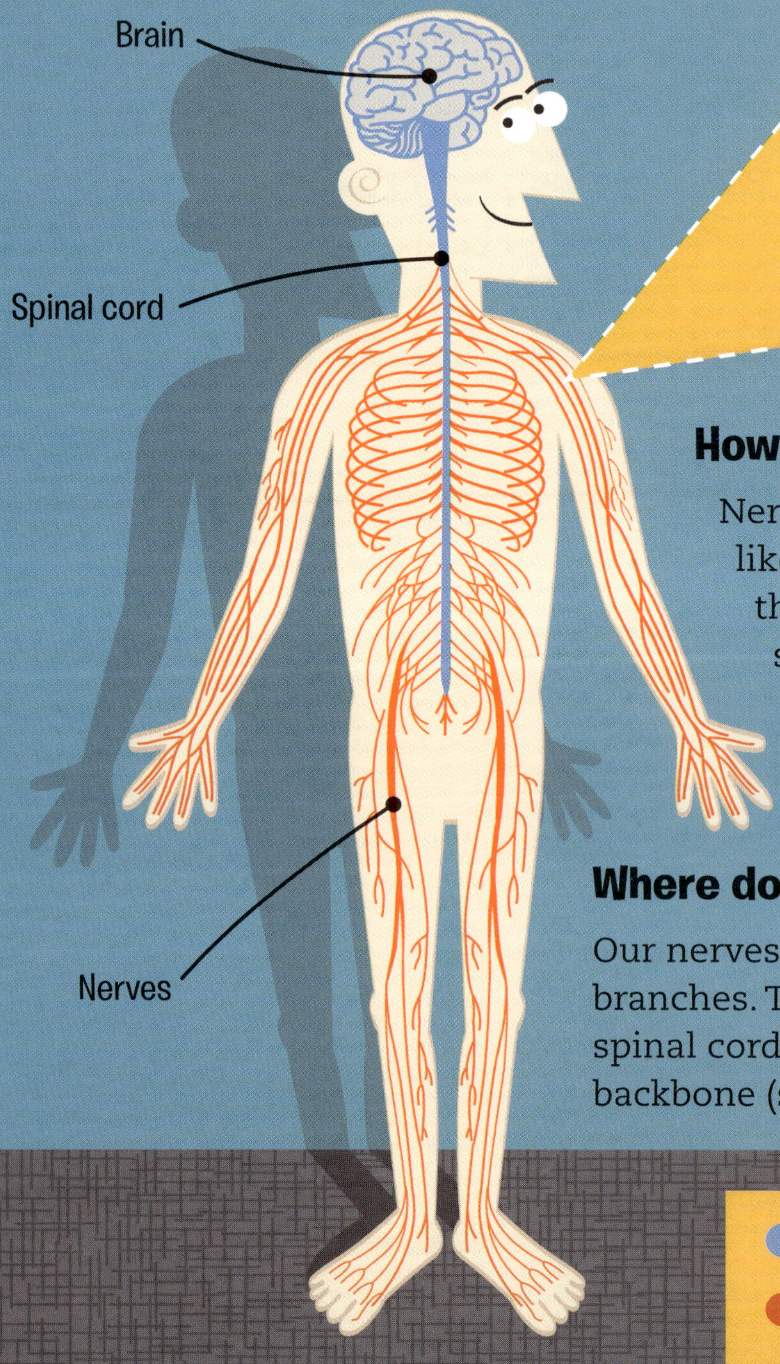

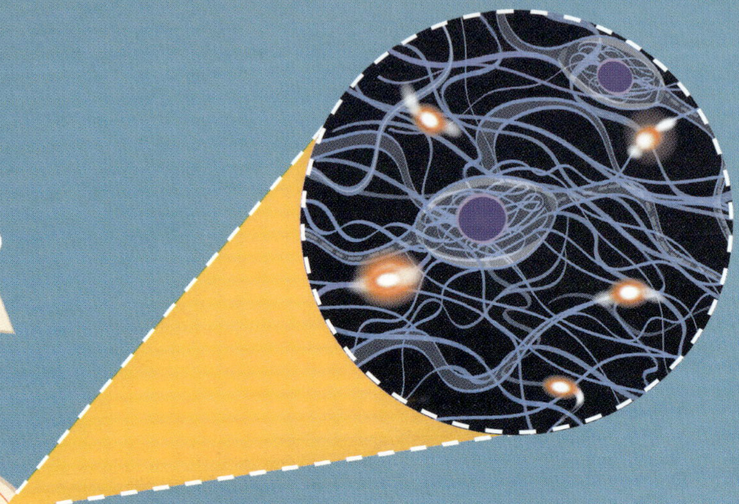

How do nerves work?

Nerves are very long, thin threads, like wires. Signals speed along them at 200 miles per hour, sending messages between your brain and other parts of your body.

Where do nerves go?

Our nerves link together like tree roots and branches. They all stretch out from your spinal cord, a big bundle of nerves in your backbone (spine) that connect to your brain.

- Central Nervous System
- Nerves

What's a nerve?

Nerves are made of special cells, called neurons. Messages to and from the brain are passed from one neuron to another, like in a relay race.

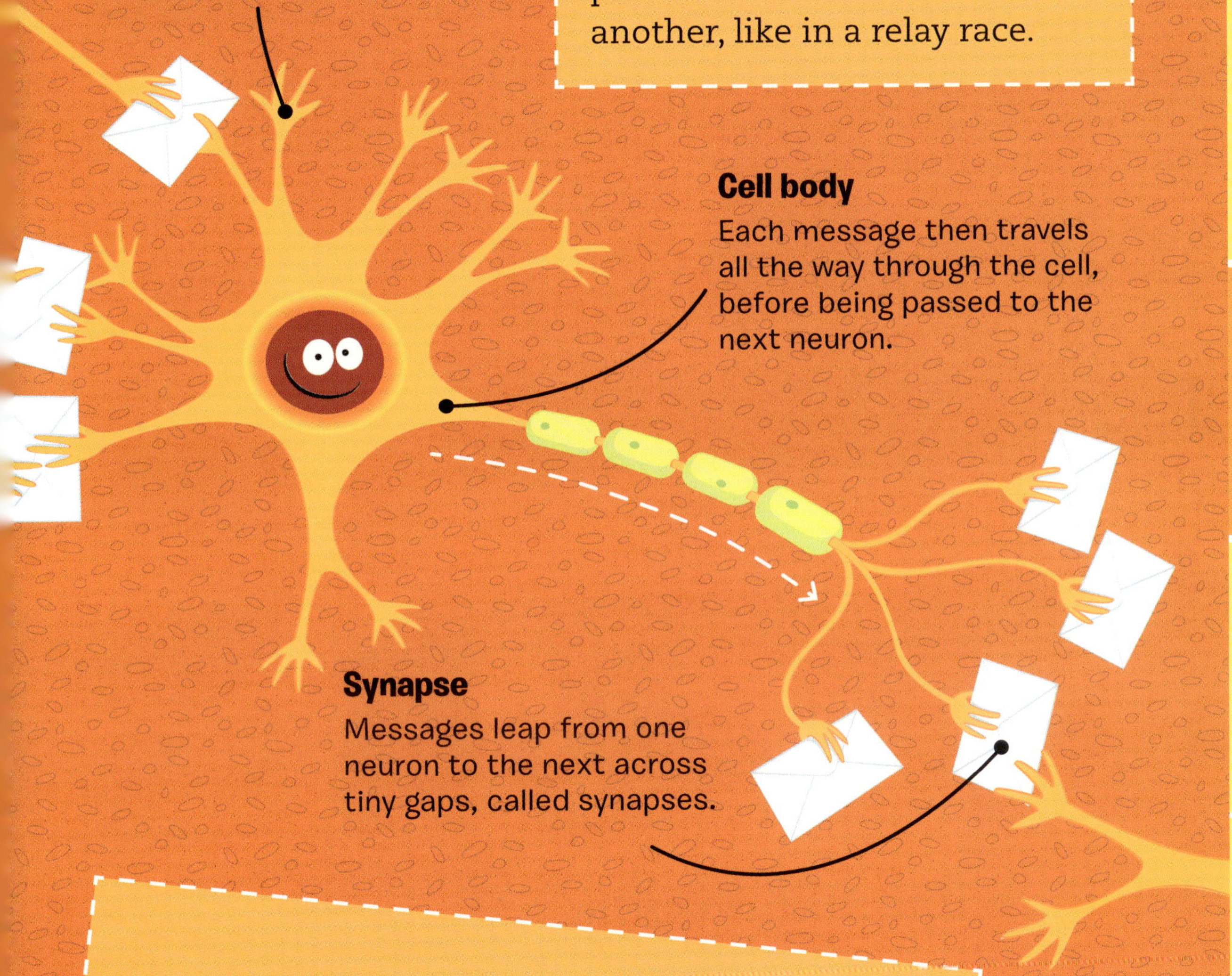

Receptors

Receptors in these branches pick up messages from other neurons.

Cell body

Each message then travels all the way through the cell, before being passed to the next neuron.

Synapse

Messages leap from one neuron to the next across tiny gaps, called synapses.

How fast are your nerves?

Your brain can send a message for your feet to start running in just 12 **milliseconds**. Phew!

WHAT MEMORIES ARE MADE OF

When you remember something, a new set of nerve connections are made through your brain, called a memory trace.

How long do memories last?

Some things we forget at once, but some memories last a lifetime.

Short-term memory

Some signals are forgotten at once. Others get passed to different parts of the brain for short-term use.

Sensory memory

Your eyes, ears and other **senses** send signals nonstop to your brain.

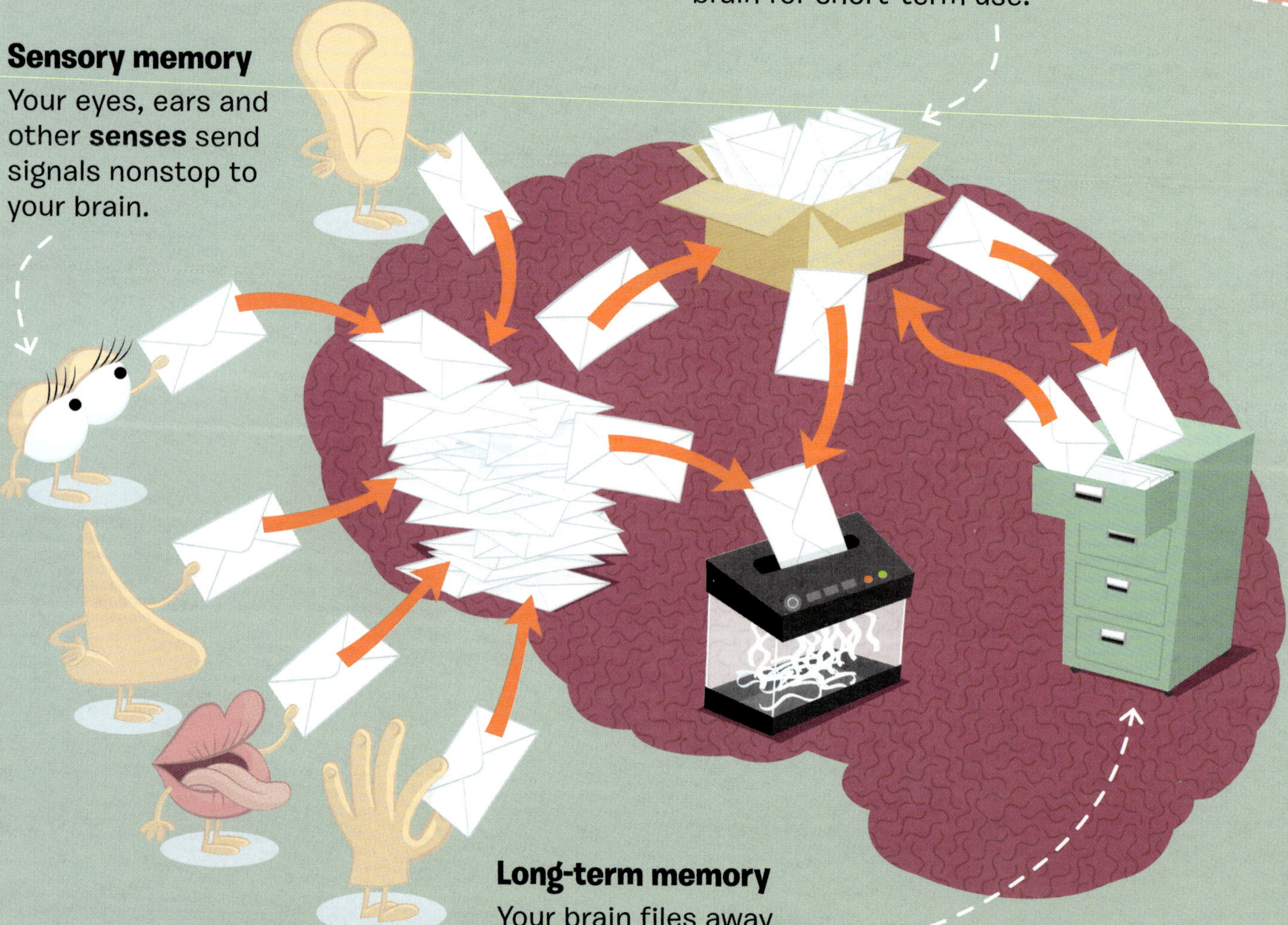

Long-term memory

Your brain files away important memories by making lasting traces.

Do we remember everything the same way?

Some things you remember instantly, such as when you scored a winning shot or goal. Experts call these explicit memories. Sometimes you have to go over things again and again, like learning a dance. These are implicit memories.

What's the world's tallest mountain?

It's Mount Everest. If you knew that, you're using your factual memory in the front left side of your brain.

FEEL IT! MOVE IT!

Have you ever wondered how your body knows when you touch things?

How do you feel touch?

Your skin is packed with feeling **sensors**, called nerve endings (because they are at the ends of your nerves).

They send signals through your sensory nerves to tell your brain what you're feeling.

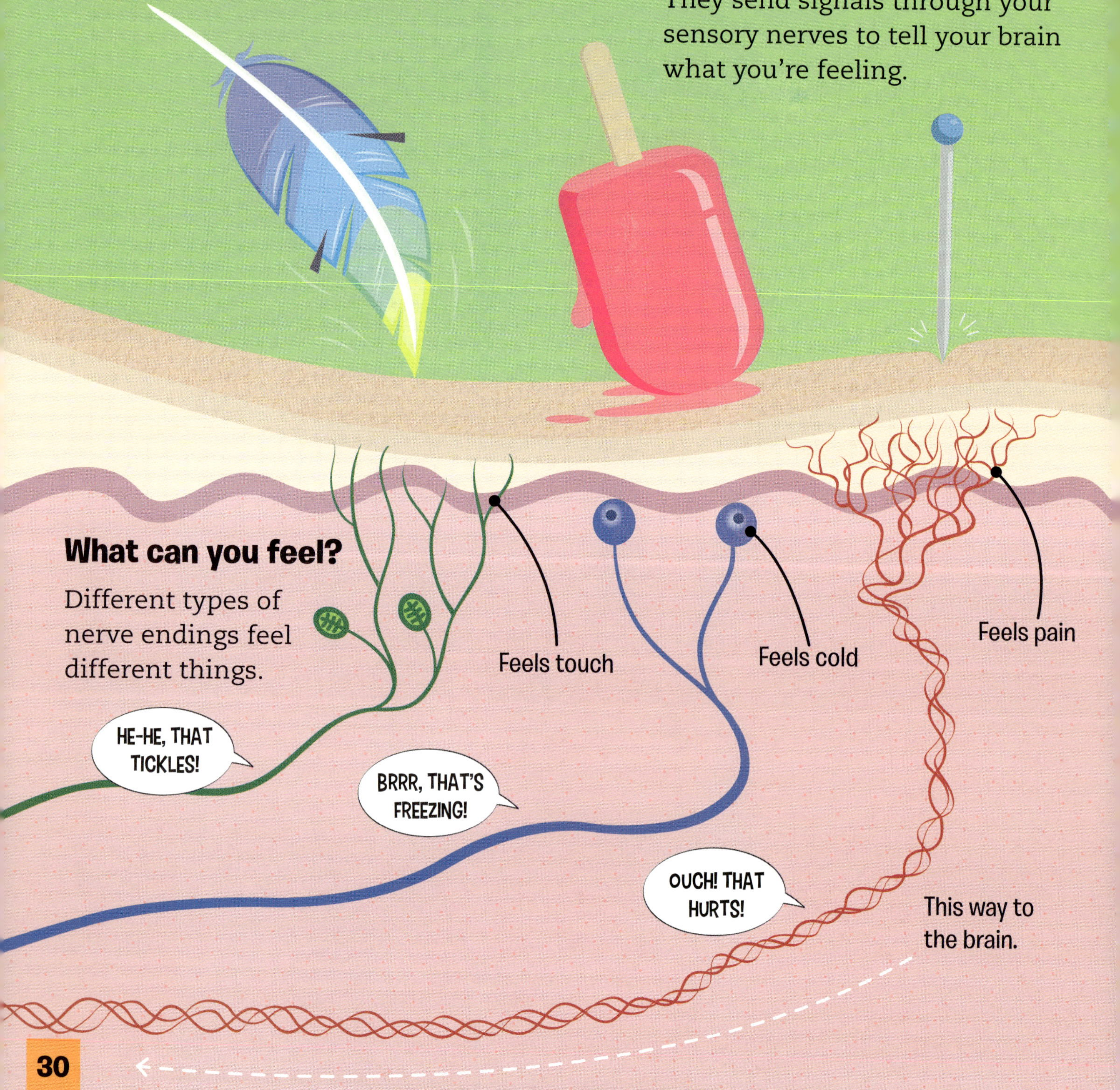

What can you feel?

Different types of nerve endings feel different things.

How do you move?

Your brain is connected to each of your muscles through nerves called motor nerves. When you think about moving, the brain sends signals to the right muscles to make it happen, just like when you pet a cat.

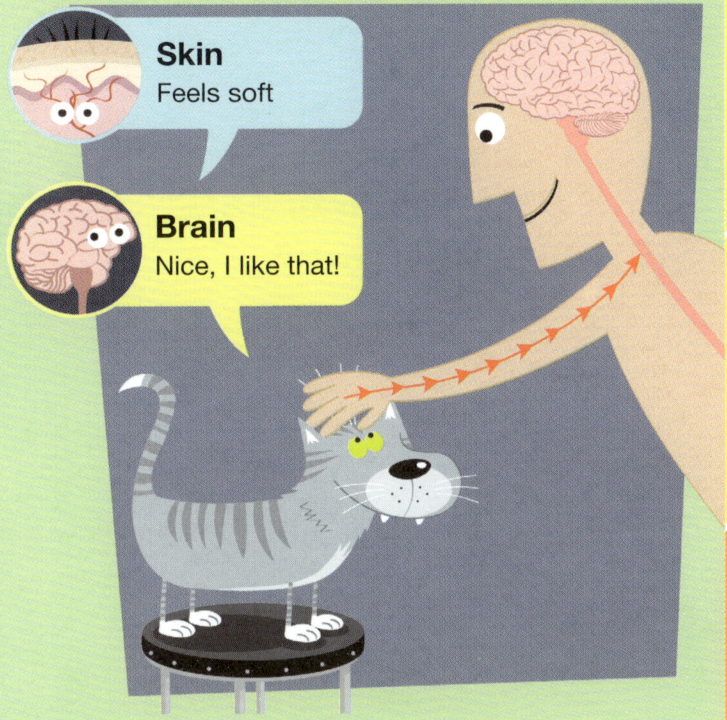

Motor Cortex

Sends out signals telling your body to move.

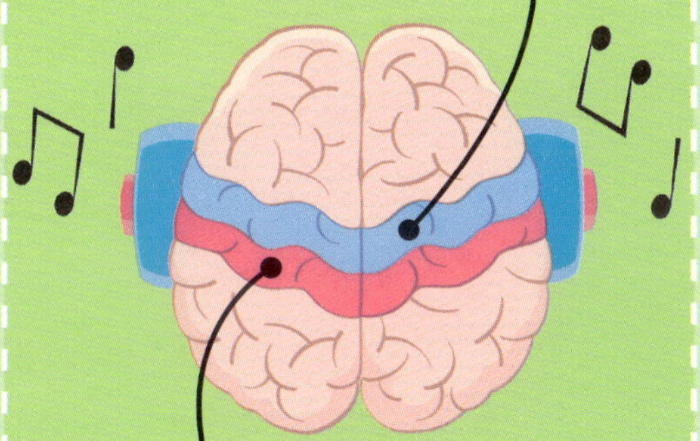

Sensory Cortex

Receives the sense signals from your body.

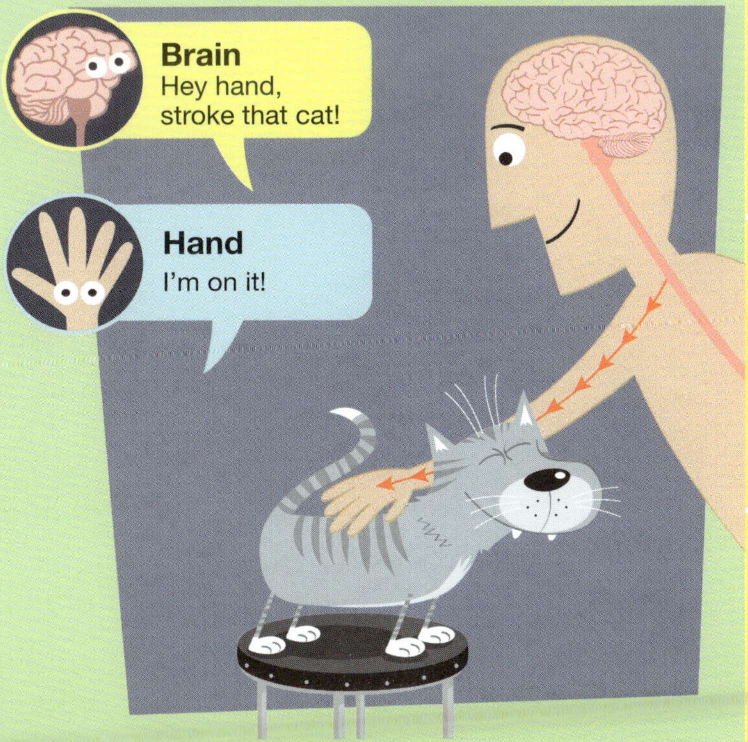

How do you control it all?

Your brain has two control panels across the top, in a band, like headphones.

MUSCLES AND BONES
ON THE SURFACE
BRAIN, NERVES AND SENSES
HEARTBEATS, BLOOD AND BREATHING
FOOD, FARTS AND DIGESTION
KEEPING WELL

EYE SPY

When you open your eyes, you can see things. It's like turning on a TV. But how do your eyes actually work?

How do your eyes see?

Each of your eyes is an amazing personal ball-shaped movie camera.

Why do we have two eyes?

Try closing one eye at a time. See the difference?

Each eye gives you a slightly different view, which together help you see the world in 3D. With just one eye, everything would look like a cardboard cut-out.

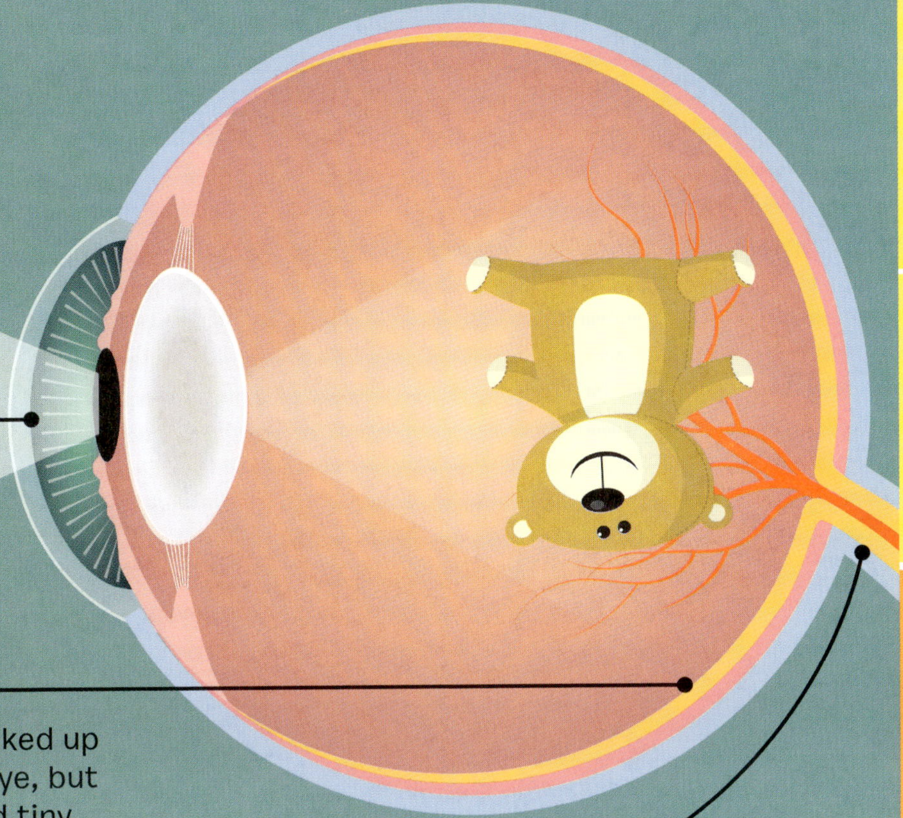

1. Cornea

This is the lens at the front that takes in the picture.

2. Retina

The picture gets picked up at the back of the eye, but it's upside down and tiny.

3. Optic nerve

This nerve sends the picture to the brain, which flips it the right way up so you can see it as it is!

We have 200 eyelashes on each eyelid to protect our eyes from dust.

Why do you blink?

Blinking is when you open and shut your eyes so fast you hardly notice. You do it every few seconds to wipe your eyes clean.

MUSCLES AND BONES
ON THE SURFACE
BRAIN, NERVES AND SENSES
HEARTBEATS, BLOOD AND BREATHING
FOOD, FARTS AND DIGESTION
KEEPING WELL

I HEAR YOU

We hear sounds with our ears, but how do they do it?

What is sound?

Sound is the air **vibrating**. You may see the vibration starting when a guitar string twangs, but most vibrations are invisible.

How do ears work?

Ears are like trumpets in reverse. They funnel sounds onto sensors inside your head.

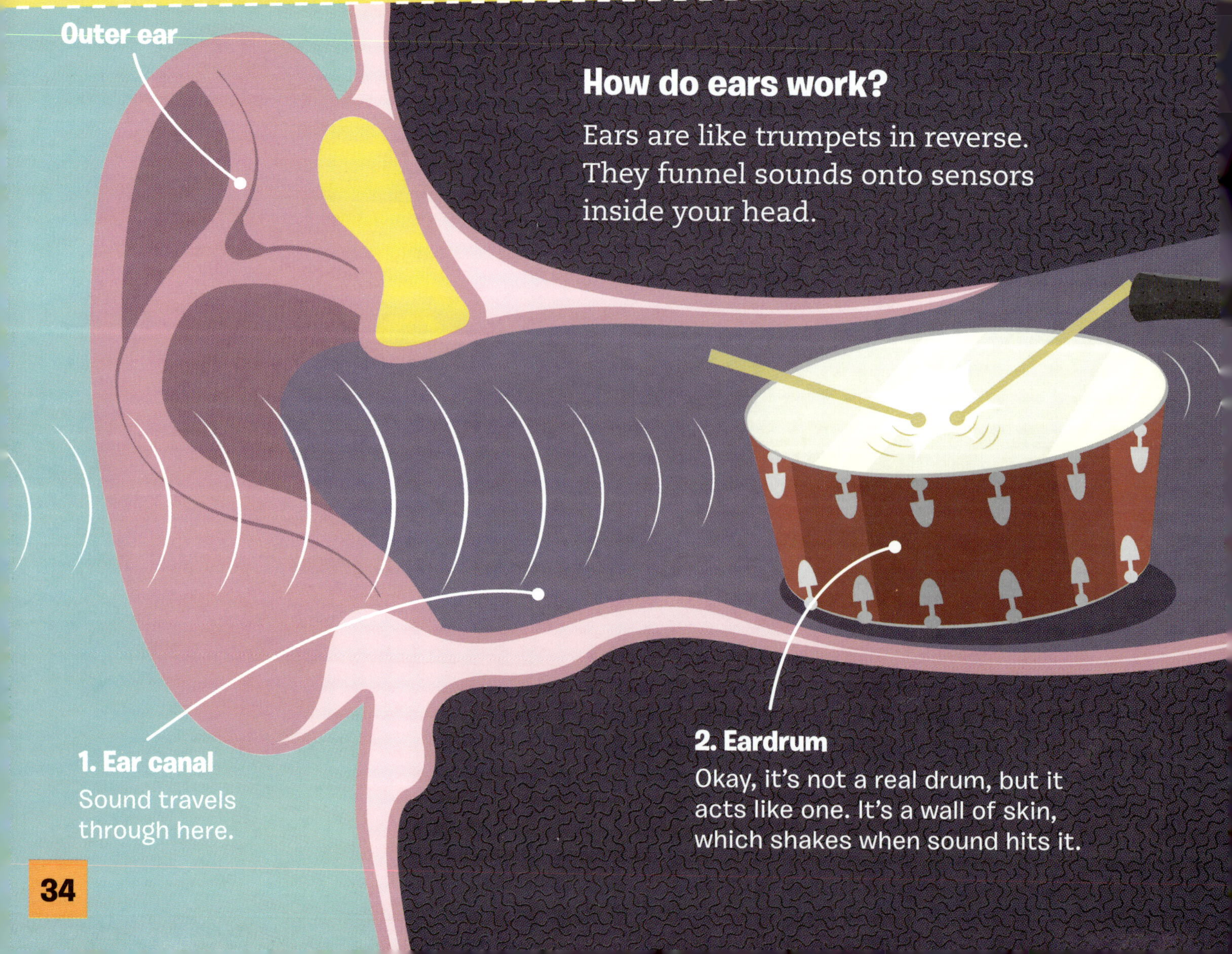

Can you hear when you're asleep?

Yes. We have to shut our eyes to sleep, but our ears go on working. Our brain ignores sounds unless they are loud or sudden.

(This is exactly what your ear looks like, 100 percent. Okay, we may have exaggerated a little!)

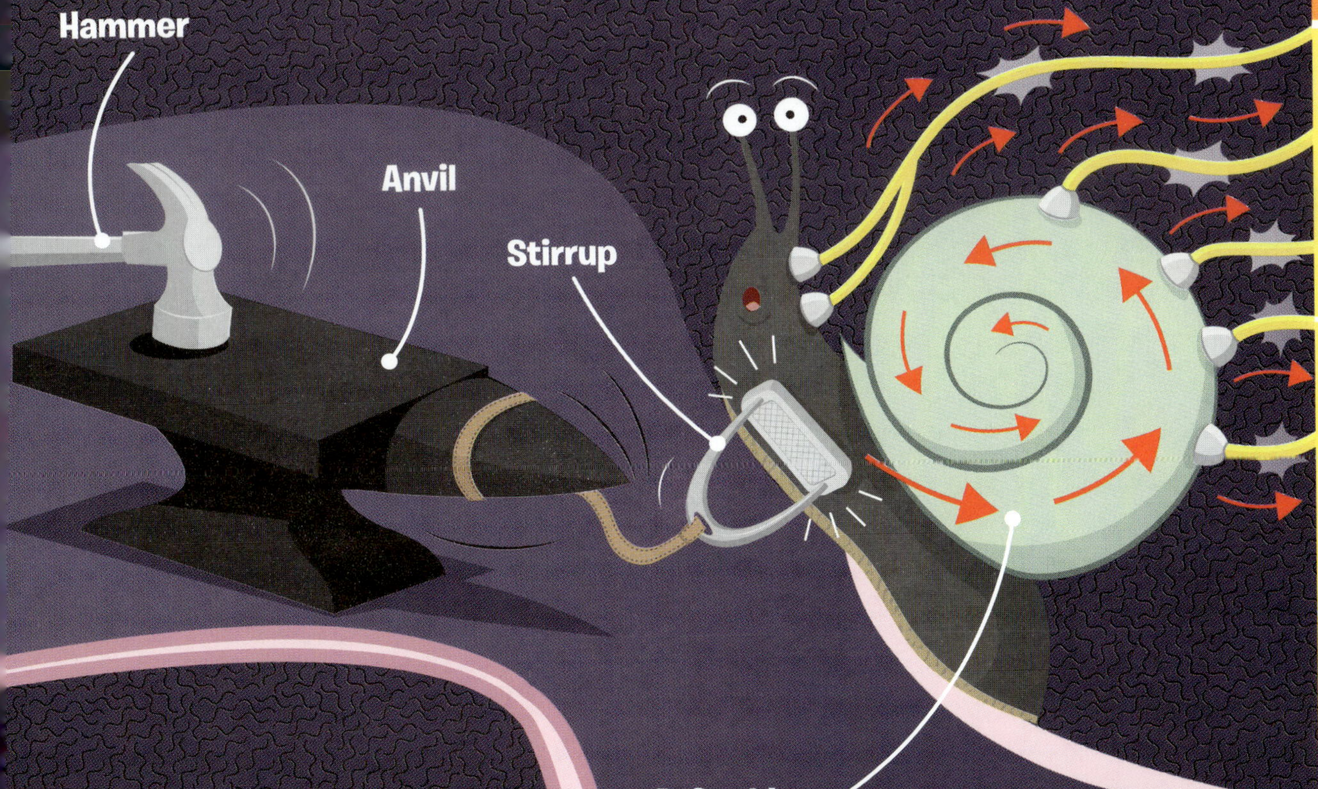

3. Ear bones

When sound shakes the drum, it rattles three bones, called the hammer, anvil and stirrup.

4. Cochlea

This looks like a snail and is filled with fluid. The rattling of the stirrup makes waves in the fluid that waggle tiny hairs, which send signals to the brain.

SMELLY AND TASTY

Smells get up your nose and tastes are on your tongue.

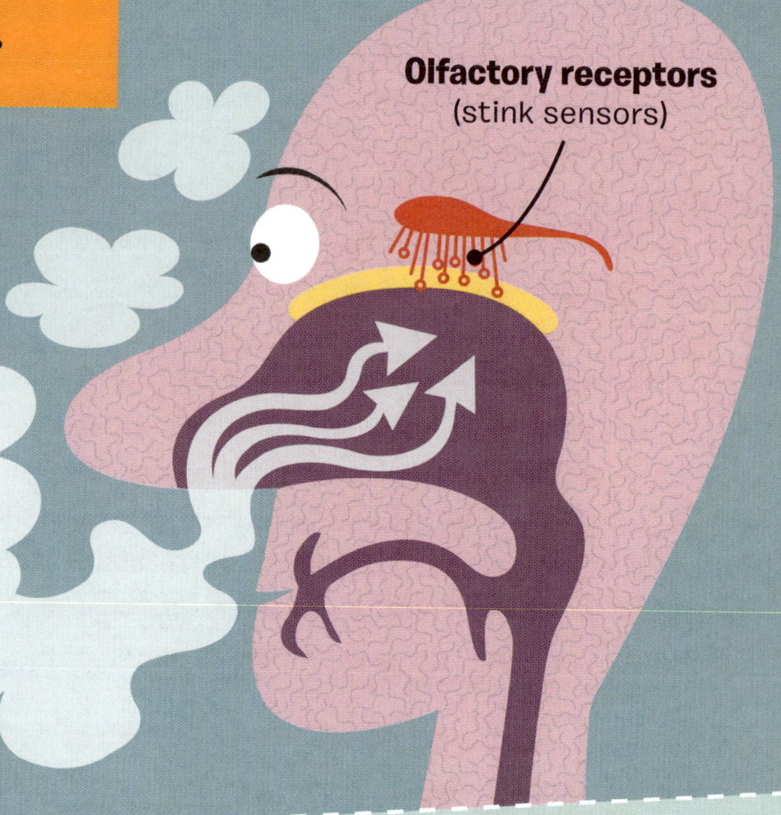

How do you smell?

The world is a very smelly place! Your nose can identify more than a trillion different smells with its bank of 350 kinds of stink sensors.

What can you smell?

Your nose is a super sensitive smell detector. In an Olympic swimming pool full of air, your nose could sniff a single stink droplet.

Do we taste with our tongues?

Yes, but that's only part of the story. Our tongues have thousands of taste sensors, called taste buds, but they can only tell if something is sweet, sour, salty, bitter or savory. We use our noses to identify the taste of individual foods.

What's the worst smell?

It's some scientists' job to make disgusting smells! Pamela Dalton made a stink bomb recipe for the U.S. military that may be the worst smell in the world. She mixed loads of gross smells together and called it Stench Soup.

MUSCLES AND BONES
ON THE SURFACE
BRAIN, NERVES AND SENSES
HEARTBEATS, BLOOD AND BREATHING
FOOD, FARTS AND DIGESTION
KEEPING WELL

SLEEPY TIME

I'm not tired at all! Why do I have to go to sleep?

Why do we sleep?

Scientists don't know for sure. They think it helps the brain recharge, like rebooting a computer.

NO SLEEP CHECKLIST:

- Your memory is terrible
- You can't think straight
- You get really moody
- You get wobbly on your feet
- You're more likely to have accidents
- You are more at risk of getting ill

What happens if you don't sleep enough?

A bad night's sleep just makes you tired and grumpy the next day. But a lot of nights without getting enough sleep will spell trouble!

What are dreams?

Dreams are stories and pictures that your brain makes up while you're asleep, like your very own private movie screening.

What happens when you go to sleep?

You go through the same four stages of sleep again and again during the night.

STAGE 1
1 to 5 minutes
You feel drowsy.

STAGE 2
5 to 60 minutes
Your brain slows and you sleep lightly.

STAGE 3
60 to 100 minutes
Your heart and breathing slow and you sleep very deeply.

STAGE 4
100 to 160 minutes
You dream a lot as your eyes flutter under the lids. This is called rapid eye movement (REM).

TAKE A DEEP BREATH

You want to know the secret of staying alive? Don't hold your breath for too long!

Why do you need to breathe?

Your body needs **oxygen**, a gas found in the air. It helps power every part of you. Without a constant supply, things quickly stop working.

What are lungs?

You have two lungs. They are big rubbery sacks containing thousands of tiny tubes, called **airways**, which branch out like a tree. Their important job (as well as breathing) is to send oxygen into your blood.

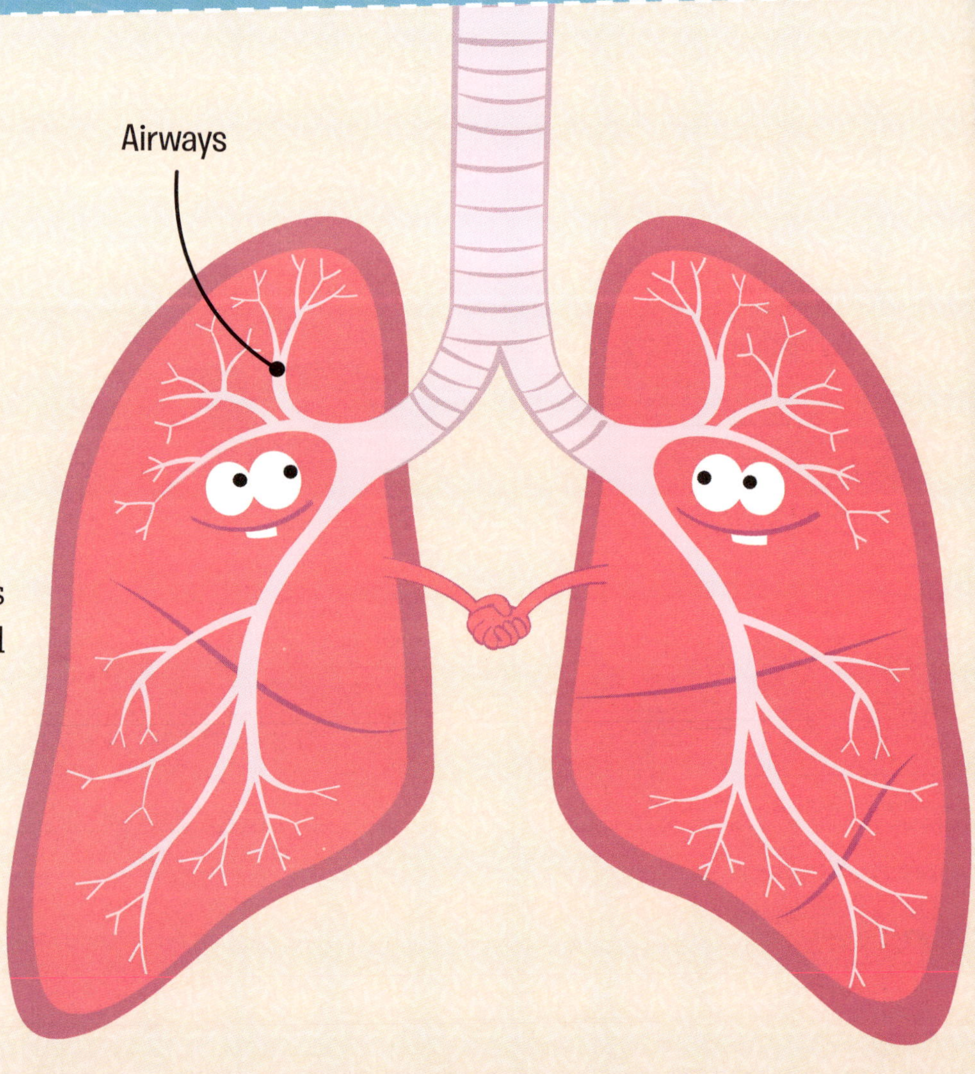

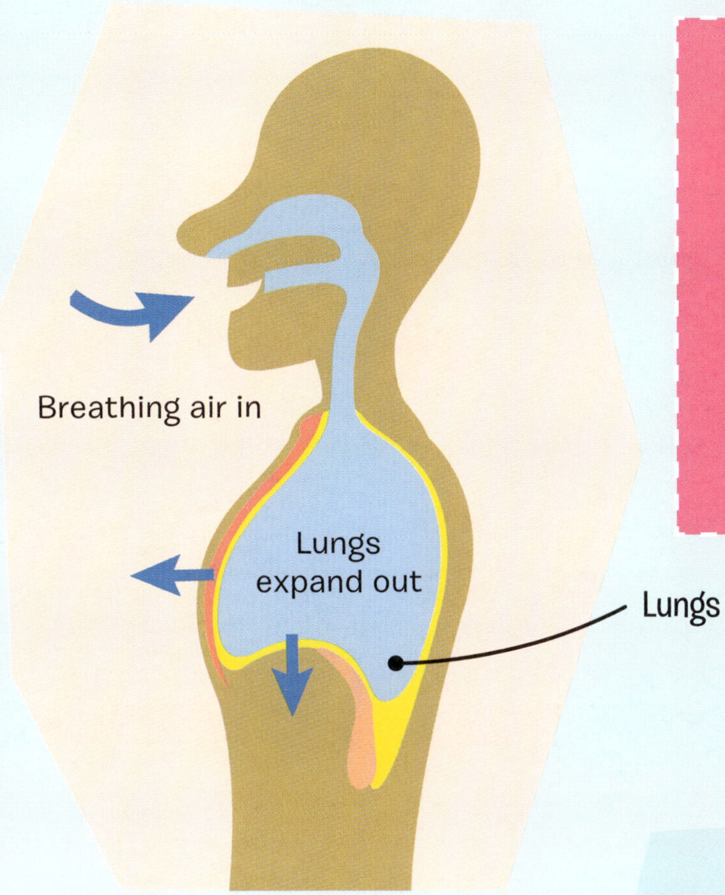

What happens when you breathe in?

When you breathe in, your lungs inflate like a balloon, sucking air in through your nose and mouth, and down into your lungs, which quickly take oxygen from it.

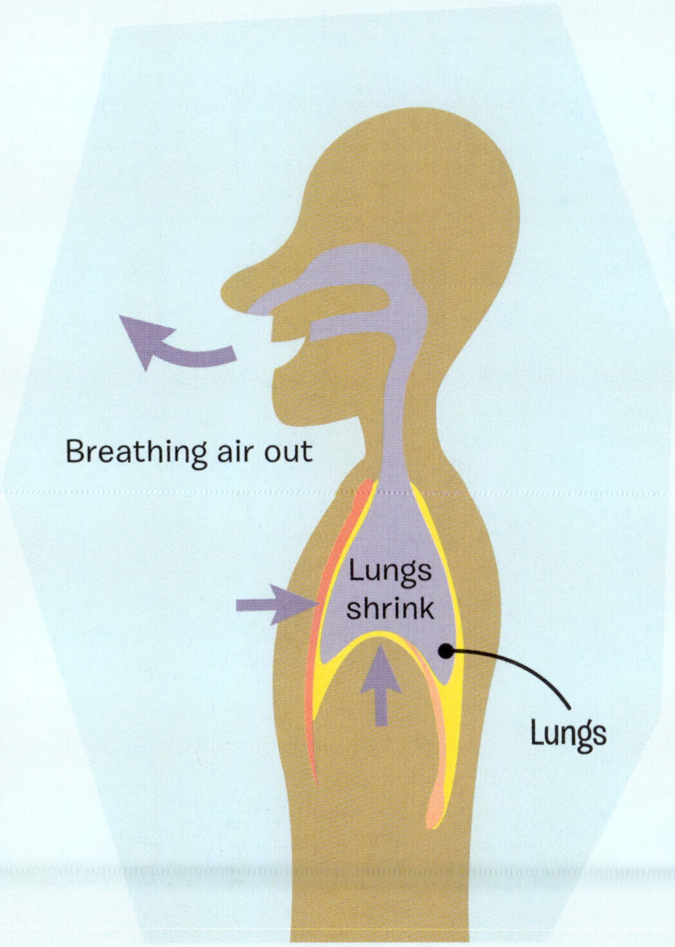

What happens when you breathe out?

To breathe out, your lungs let the air go again, along with unwanted carbon dioxide, a gas made by your body.

MUSCLES AND BONES
ON THE SURFACE
BRAIN, NERVES AND SENSES
HEARTBEATS, BLOOD AND BREATHING
FOOD, FARTS AND DIGESTION
KEEPING WELL

KEEP THE BEAT

Press your fingers on the middle of your chest. Can you feel your heart beating?

What is your heart?

Your heart is a little pump in the middle of your chest. It's made of muscle that tightens and relaxes all the time to pump blood around your body.

How does your heart work?

When your heart muscle relaxes, blood rushes in. When the muscle tightens it pushes blood out.

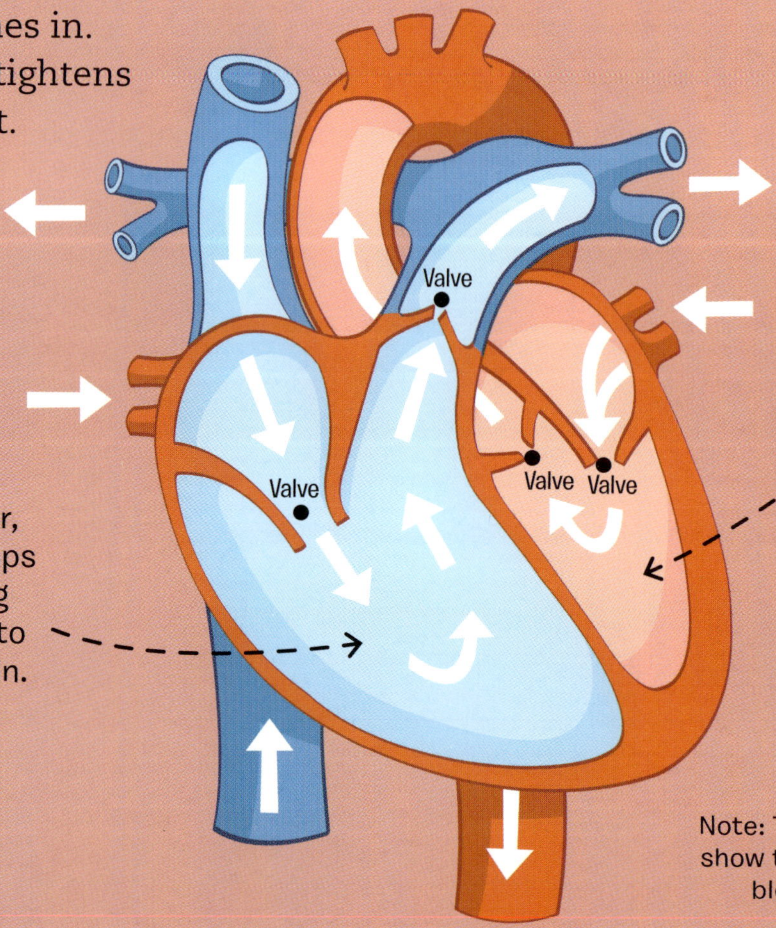

1. The big, strong, left side pumps blood out around the body.

2. The smaller, right side pumps the returning blood back into the heart again.

Note: The white arrows show the direction the blood flows in.

Why can you hear your heartbeat?

Every time blood is pushed out, little flaps inside your heart, called valves, slam shut like doors to stop it from flowing back the wrong way. The thumping noise of your heartbeat is the sound of the valves slamming shut.

How fast does your heart beat?

Your heart normally beats about 75 times a minute. But when you run, it starts pumping faster to supply your muscles with the extra oxygen they need.

You can feel each little push, or pulse, of your blood, by touching the inside of your wrist. You could even try counting how many beats you feel in a minute.

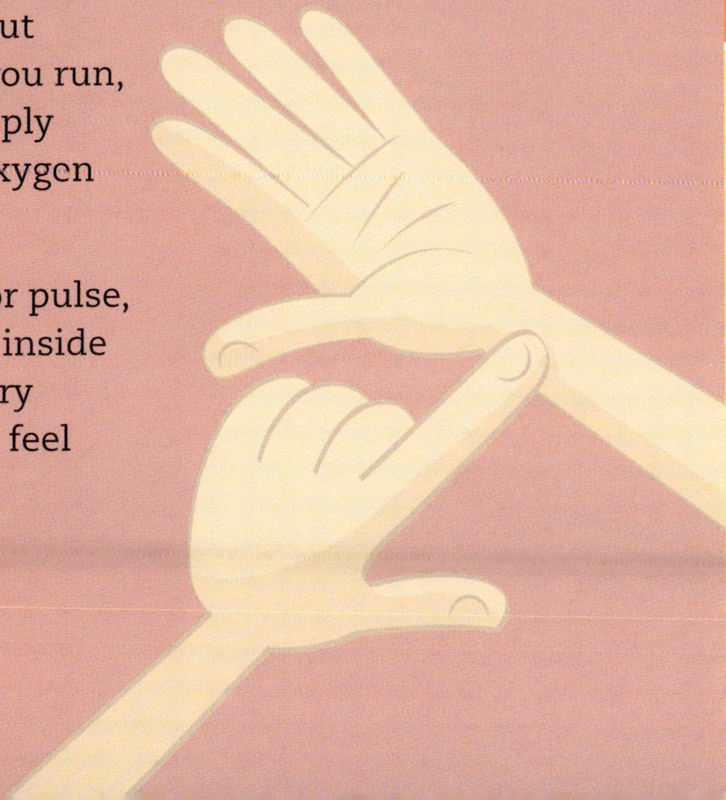

BLOOD CAROUSEL

Your body is full of a red liquid called blood, but what's it for?

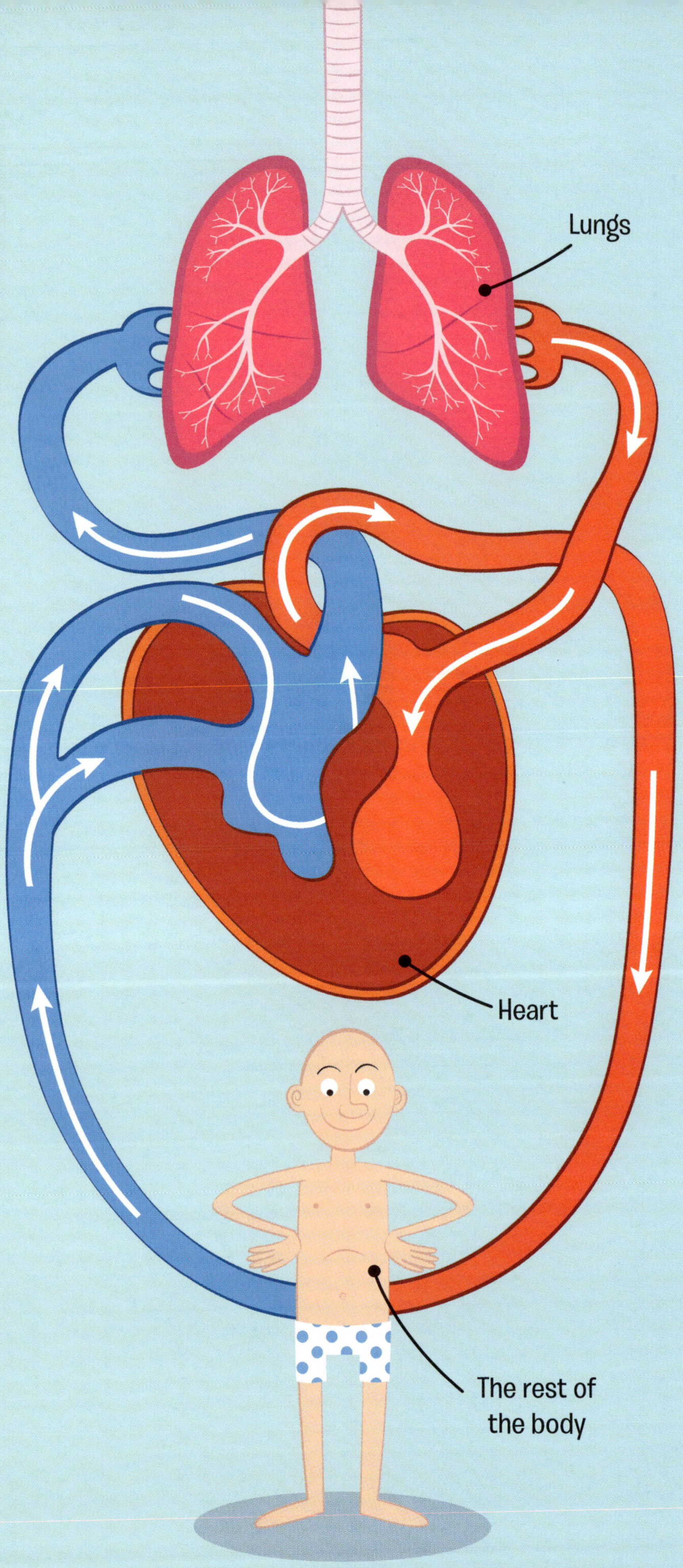

What does blood do?

Its main job is to carry oxygen from your lungs to every part of your body. Your heart pumps it around through pipes called blood vessels. This is called circulation.

- **Out**: Blood carries oxygen from the lungs to the body.
- **Back**: Blood carries unwanted carbon dioxide waste back to the lungs.

What are arteries and veins?

These are the biggest blood vessels. Arteries carry blood loaded with oxygen away from the lungs. Veins carry blood back. The oxygen makes the blood in arteries bright red.

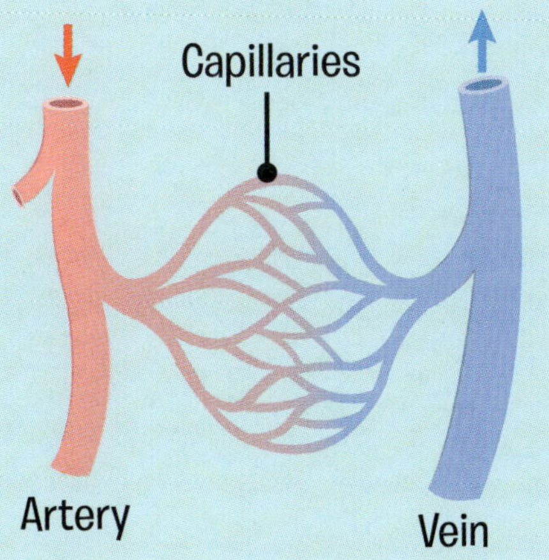

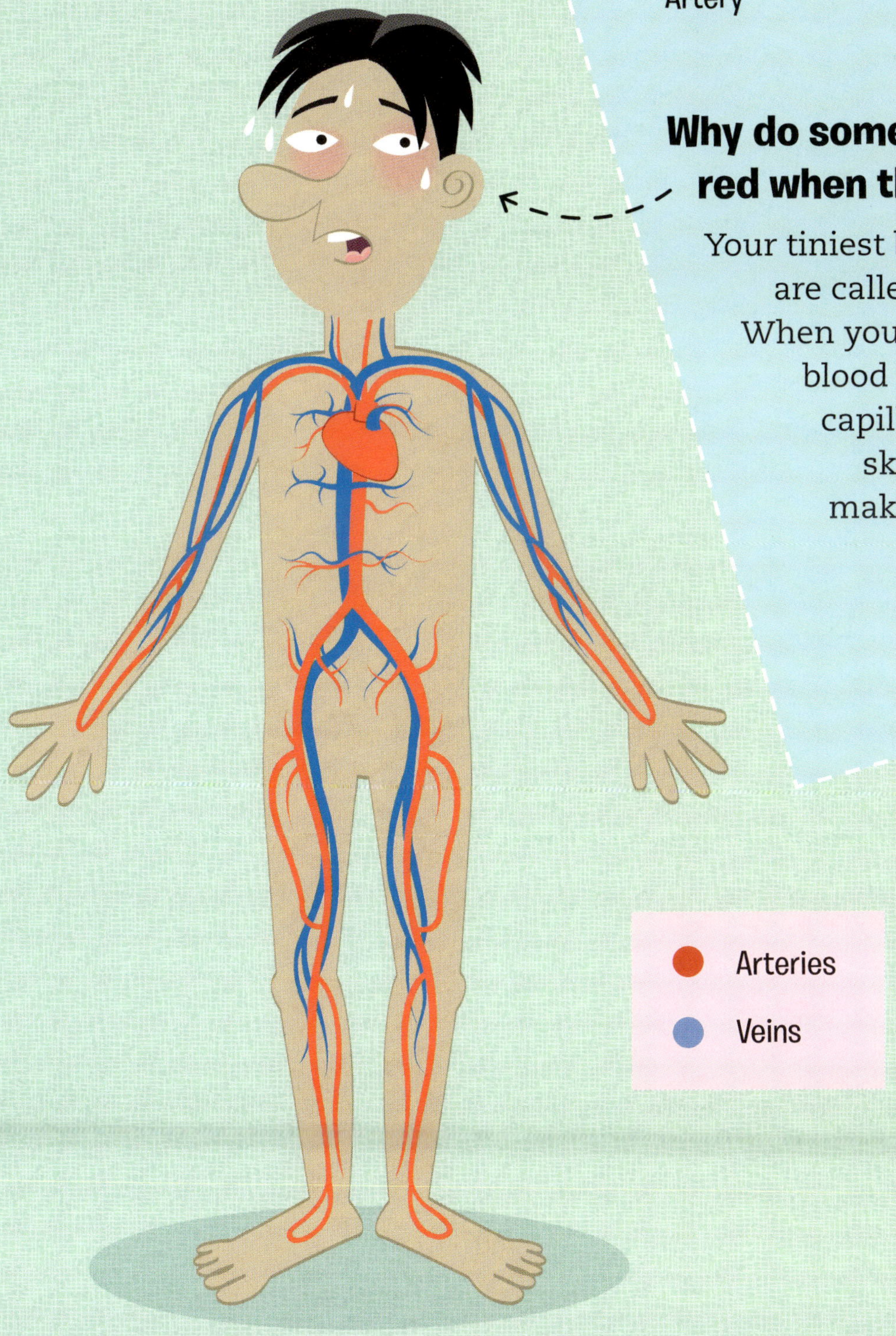

Why do some people go red when they're hot?

Your tiniest blood vessels are called capillaries. When you're hot, more blood runs into the capillaries in your skin to cool off, making your skin look redder.

LIFE JUICE

Blood looks just like red ink, doesn't it? But what is it really made of?

What's in blood?

Your blood is like a soup full of useful substances that need to be carried around the body.

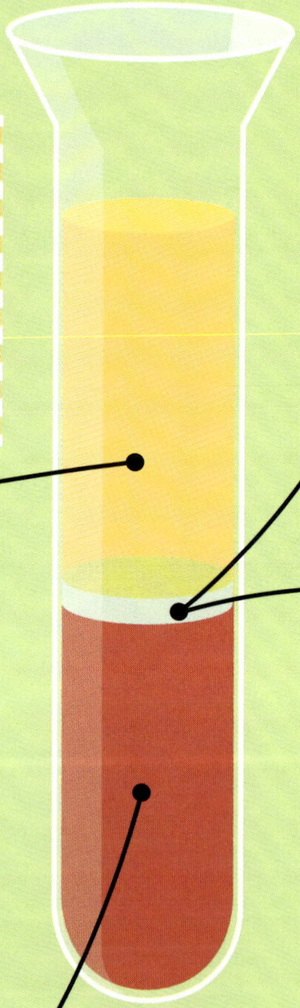

White blood cells

They help your body fight germs.

Plasma

It is the watery part of your blood.

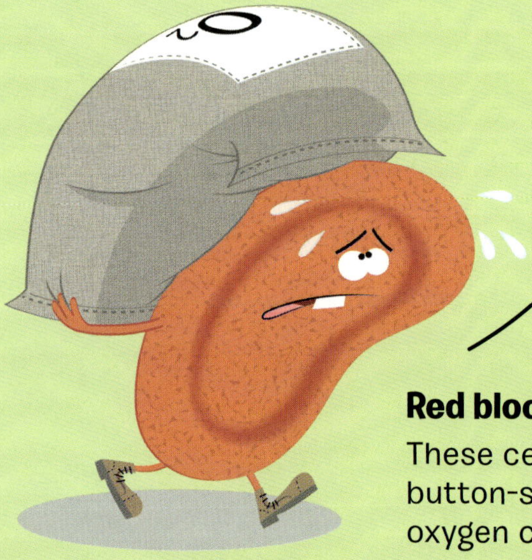

Platelets

They are the emergency team for fixing any damage.

Red blood cells

These cells are button-shaped oxygen carriers.

How much blood do you have?

The average adult has enough blood in their body to fill about 15 to 16 cans of cola.

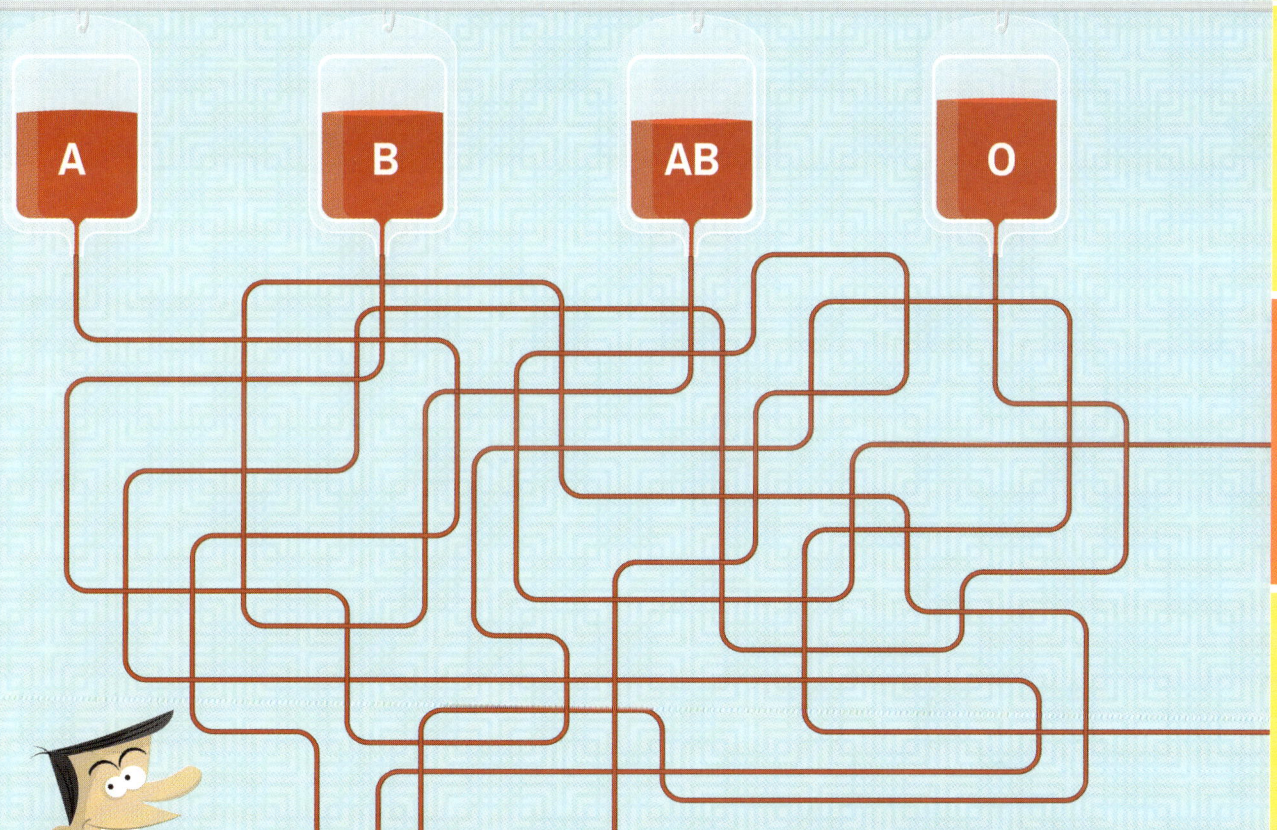

Is everyone's blood the same?

No. Your blood belongs to one of four different groups: A, B, AB or O. If you need to be given blood in hospital in an emergency, it must belong to your own blood group.

MUSCLES AND BONES
ON THE SURFACE
BRAIN, NERVES AND SENSES
HEARTBEATS, BLOOD AND BREATHING
FOOD, FARTS AND DIGESTION
KEEPING WELL

WHAT A MOUTHFUL!

Most of us just love stuffing our mouths with food. But just what goes on in there?

What do your teeth do?

Your food gets mashed to a pulp between your teeth. You have about 32 teeth, and each one has a coat of **enamel**, the body's toughest substance.

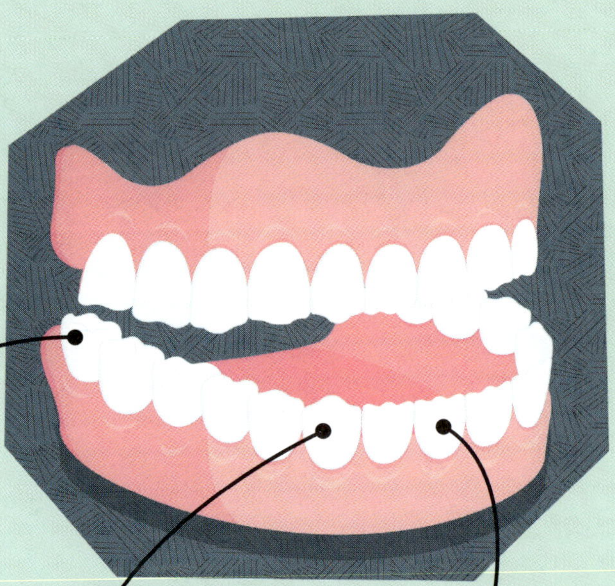

Molars
These teeth, at the back, are big crushers and mashers.

Canines
These teeth, at the side, are rippers.

Incisors
These teeth, at the front, are sharp choppers and slicers.

Why must we clean our teeth?

If you don't clean your teeth every day, they will soon be coated in a sticky goo called plaque, which contains a lot of **bacteria** (see page 68). Yuck! These bacteria ooze chemicals that can rot your tooth enamel.

Why does yummy food make you drool?

Liquid saliva in your mouth helps soften food. When you smell something nice, your brain tells your salivary glands to start oozing saliva into your mouth.

Chemicals in saliva, called enzymes, help turn food mushy.

It also contains chemicals that heal cuts and look after your teeth.

GOT TO EAT

Food can be really yummy, but that's not the only reason we eat it.

What's food for?

Like filling a car with fuel, eating food gives you energy to move and help you stay warm. Food also gives stuff you need for growing and staying well.

Carbohydrates

Sugary and starchy foods are great energy fuel for your body.

Fats

Your body stores fat from food to use as emergency energy.

Protein

Most of your body is made from materials called proteins. But you can't make them all. That's why you need to eat foods with proteins to stay healthy.

What are vitamins and minerals?

Vitamins and minerals are super substances that are found in the food we eat. Different foods contain specific vitamins and minerals that help different parts of your body stay healthy.

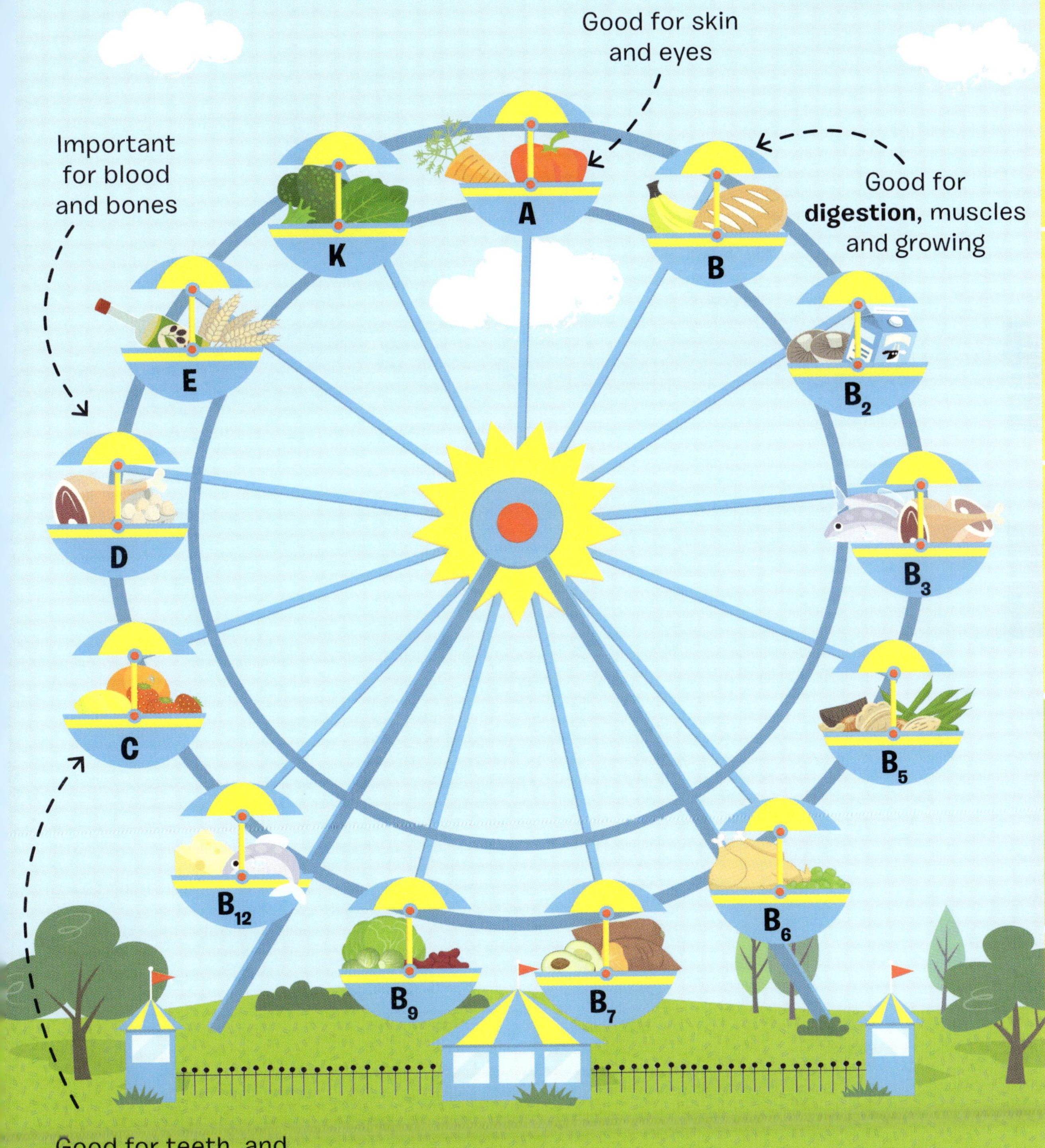

(Note: Vitamins are named with letters of the alphabet. But, just to confuse us all, there are a lot of different B vitamins.)

MUSCLES AND BONES

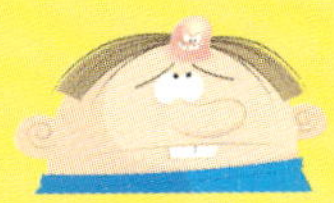

ON THE SURFACE

BRAIN, NERVES AND SENSES

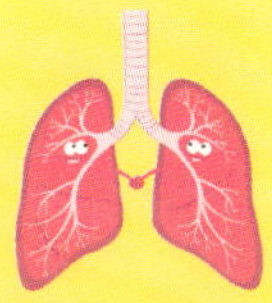

HEARTBEATS, BLOOD AND BREATHING

FOOD, FARTS AND DIGESTION

KEEPING WELL

BELLY BUSINESS

Have you ever wondered what happens to your food after you've swallowed it?

Where does food go?

Down your throat and into your stomach. When it's empty, your stomach is tiny. But when food arrives, it swells up like a balloon.

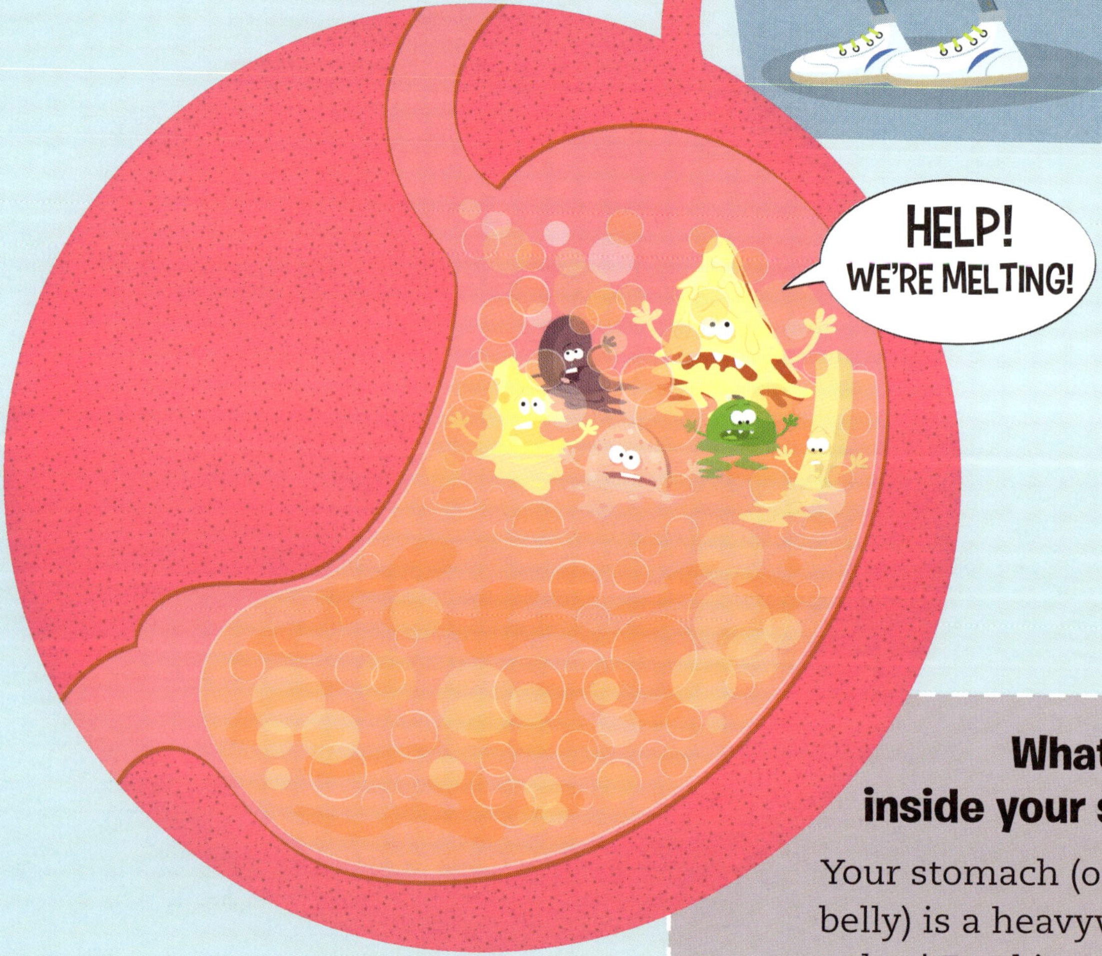

What happens inside your stomach?

Your stomach (or tummy or belly) is a heavyweight food masher! Food is attacked in it with powerful juices and crushed to a pulp by squeezing muscles.

What's vomit?

Vomit is mushed-up food from your stomach, along with its slimy lining, saliva and stomach juices.

What makes you throw up?

If your stomach is upset, the "vomit spot" in your brain tells some stomach muscles to open and others to squeeze from below, then whoosh, up it comes through your mouth. Yuck!

Why do you burp?

Burps are the sounds you make when gas escapes from your stomach through your mouth. Every day, you burp enough gas to fill a 34-fluid ounce (1-litre) bottle.

YOU'VE GOT GUTS

We've all got guts, gurgling away inside us. That's where your food goes. But why do you need guts?

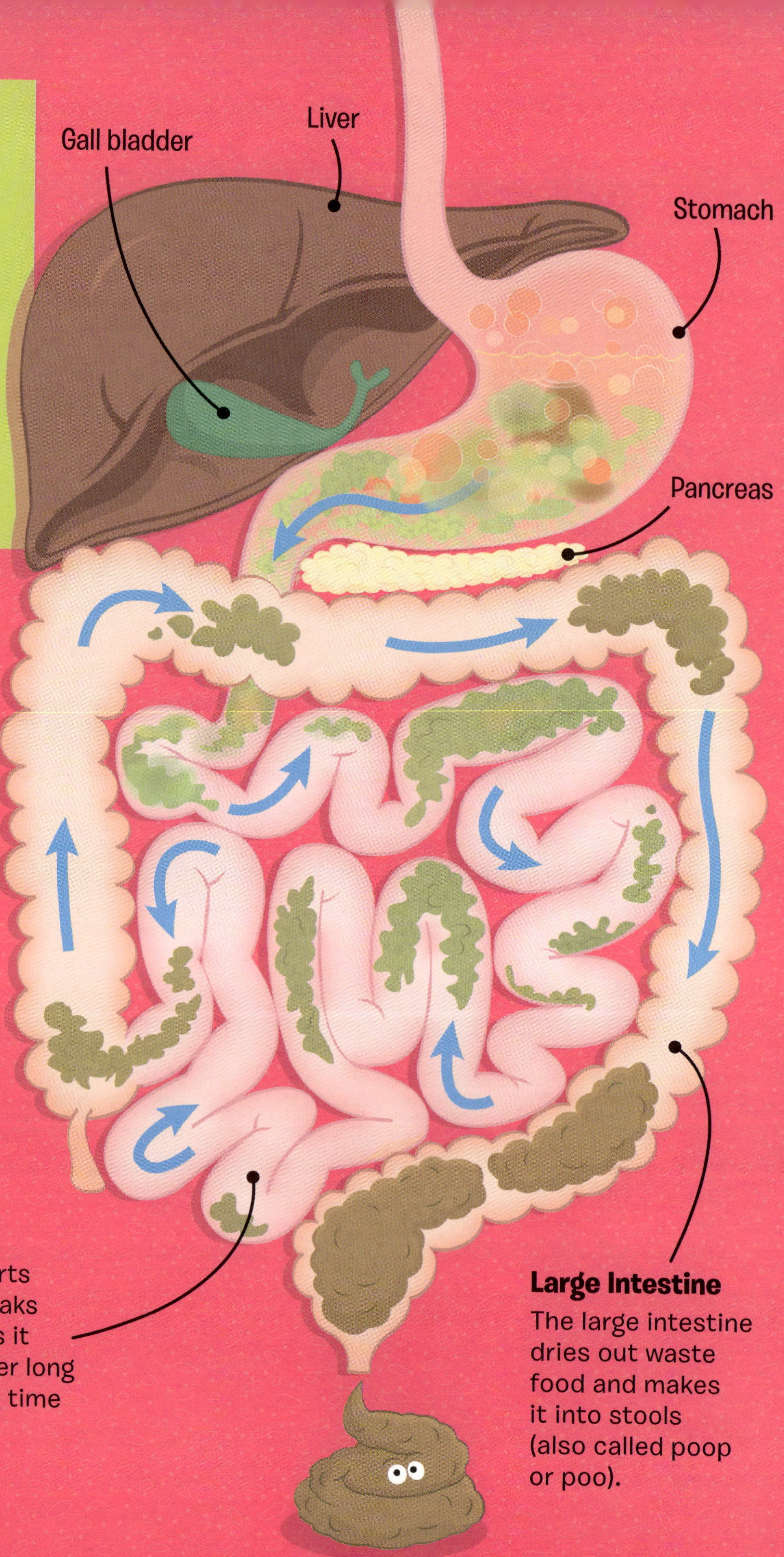

What are guts?

They're a super-long tunnel twisted around inside you, called the digestive tract. There's a thin part called the small intestine and a fat one called the large intestine.

Small Intestine

The small intestine starts at your stomach. It breaks down food and absorbs it into your body. It's super long because it takes a long time to break food down.

Large Intestine

The large intestine dries out waste food and makes it into stools (also called poop or poo).

How long does it take food to travel through your body?

Food working its way through your body is called digestion. How long it takes depends on what you've eaten, but it's usually between 2 and 5 days.

It takes 8 seconds for food to get to your stomach.

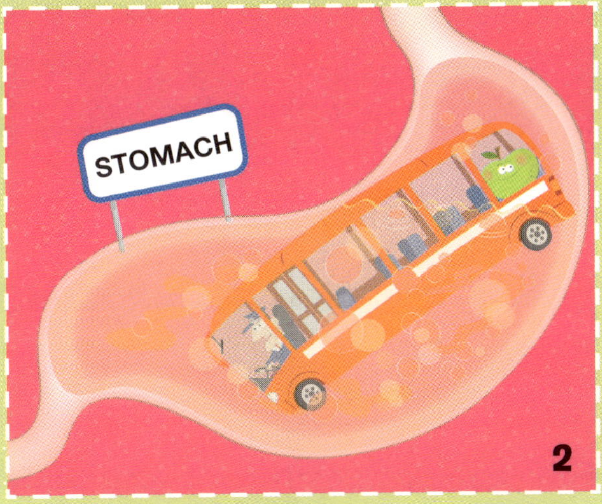

Food spends 2 to 4 hours in your stomach.

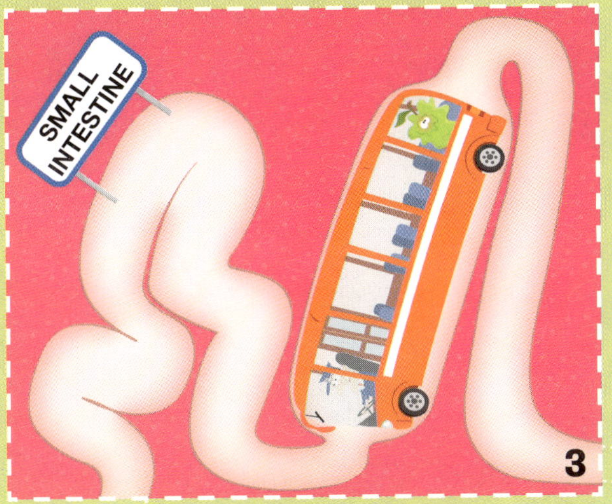

It takes 3 to 5 hours to get through your small intestine.

What's left in the large intestine can hang around for about 36 hours!

BUSY LIVER

Food is full of all kinds of useful ingredients. But how does your body get them working for you?

What does your liver do?

Your liver is your own personal factory for turning the useful ingredients that your intestines took from your food into substances your body can use.

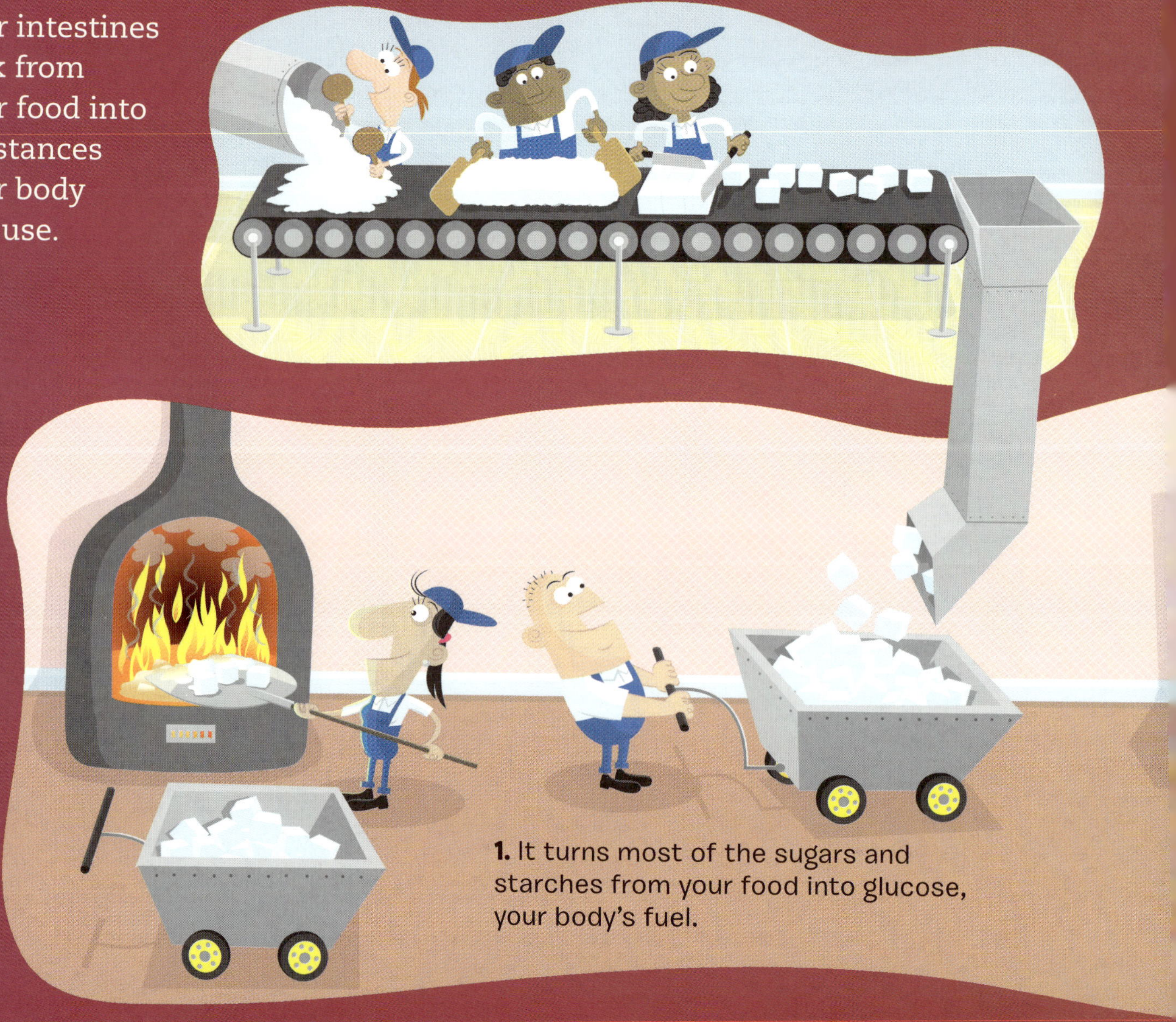

1. It turns most of the sugars and starches from your food into glucose, your body's fuel.

Is that all your liver does?

No. Your liver is a super multitasker with a lot of jobs, including . . .

. . . storing vitamins and minerals . . .

. . . making new liquid for your blood, called plasma . . .

. . . making bile, a yellowish liquid that it sends to the intestines to help break down food . . .

. . . and that's just to start. It can even regrow itself! What a smart organ!

2. It also stores some as an emergency fuel supply, called glycogen.

3. It packages any leftovers into fat and sends it around your body.

MUSCLES AND BONES

ON THE SURFACE

BRAIN, NERVES AND SENSES

HEARTBEATS, BLOOD AND BREATHING

FOOD, FARTS AND DIGESTION

KEEPING WELL

BETTER OUT THAN IN!

Everyone uses the toilet and farts! But, have you ever wondered why?

Why do we poop?

Not everything in the food we eat can be used by the body. The leftover waste at the end of the digestion process comes out as stools (or faeces), which we call poop or poo.

What's in a stool?

A stool contains:

Bacteria
Don't worry, these are good bacteria that help with digestion and keep you healthy.

Water

Bile
A yellow liquid made in the liver that breaks down fat.

Fiber
Foods have fiber (or fibre) that can help food move smoothly through the digestive system, but it doesn't break down itself.

What is a fart?

A fart is a mixture of gases that form as your food breaks down inside you. These gases need to go somewhere, so they come out as smelly farts!

Why do they smell bad?

Some gases have a scent. The different gases that form a fart can be pretty smelly when they are combined together!

MUSCLES AND BONES
ON THE SURFACE
BRAIN, NERVES AND SENSES
HEARTBEATS, BLOOD AND BREATHING
FOOD, FARTS AND DIGESTION
KEEPING WELL

WHEN YOU'VE GOT TO GO . . .

We all have to pee a few times a day, sometimes at very awkward moments. What's that all about?

What's in your pee?

The proper name for pee is urine. It is mostly water, but small amounts of other things get flushed out with it.

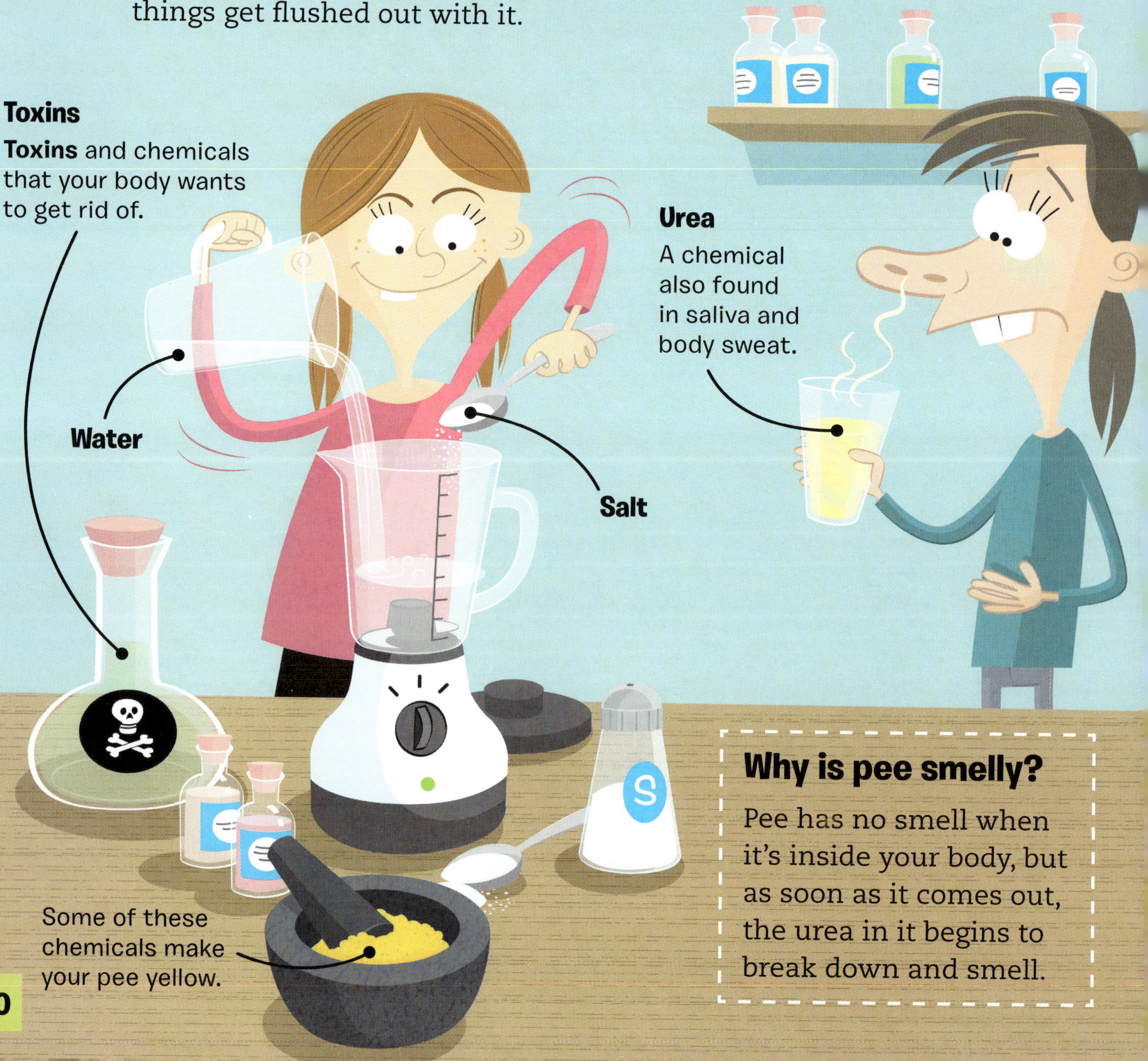

Why is pee smelly?

Pee has no smell when it's inside your body, but as soon as it comes out, the urea in it begins to break down and smell.

Why do we pee?

You take in water all the time by eating and drinking. So, you have to pee to keep the amount of water in your body just right.

Why does water matter?

Your body is mostly made of water. It's amazing you don't slosh around when you walk! You need to drink plenty of water to keep everything in your body working properly.

HOT STUFF

Your body is like a little heater, which is why your bed feels warm in the morning. So, why are we warm?

How do you keep warm?

Your body's heat comes from the food you eat. Your liver and body cells are like little stoves turning the energy stored in sugar into heat. Putting on extra clothes helps, too!

How do you keep cool?

You keep cool mostly by breathing out. That's why your breath is warm. You also lose heat through your skin, which is why you wear less clothes in hot weather. Sweating helps, too!

Why's your body hot?

Cakes need to be cooked at the right temperature to bake well, right? Well, your body has to stay at the right temperature to work properly, too. Around 98.6°F (37°C) is perfect.

If it gets too hot or too cold, you get ill.

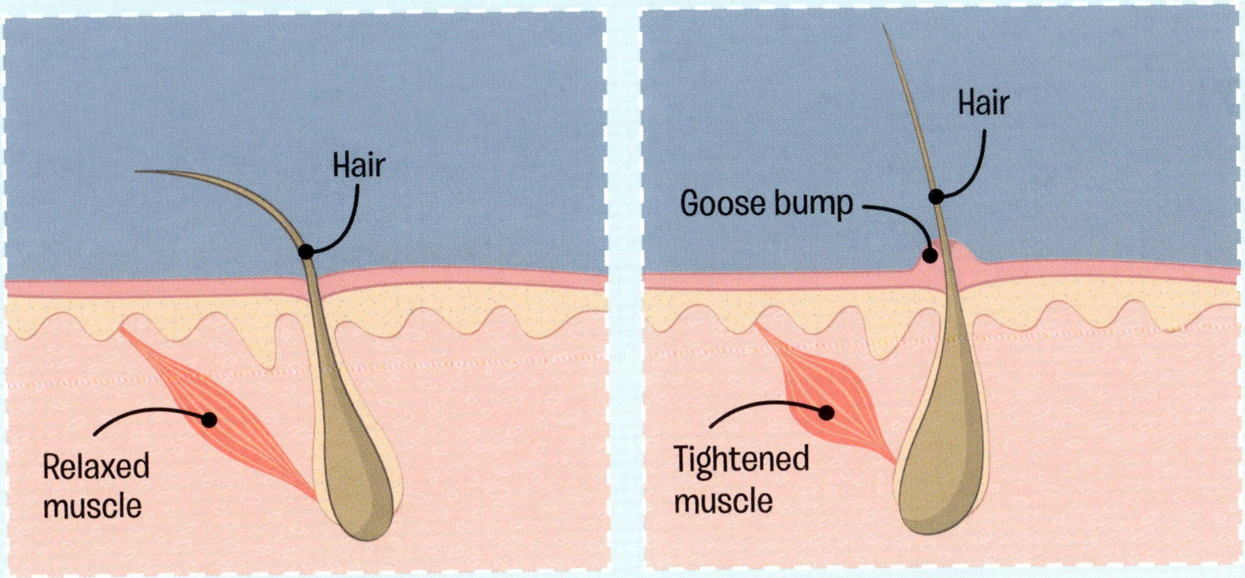

What are goosebumps?

When you're cold, your skin may get goosebumps. These happen when little muscles under your skin make your hairs stand up to try and trap a layer of warm air, like furry animals do.

GETTING SICK

Being sick is never fun. What actually makes you ill?

What are germs?

Germs are **microbes** that are so small they're basically invisible! They may be tiny, but when they get into your body, they can multiply and make you sick. The main germs are bacteria and viruses.

What are bacteria?

Bacteria are tiny living things made from just one cell. Millions are harmless, but there are a few that are really bad news! Here are some mean ones and some of the diseases they cause:

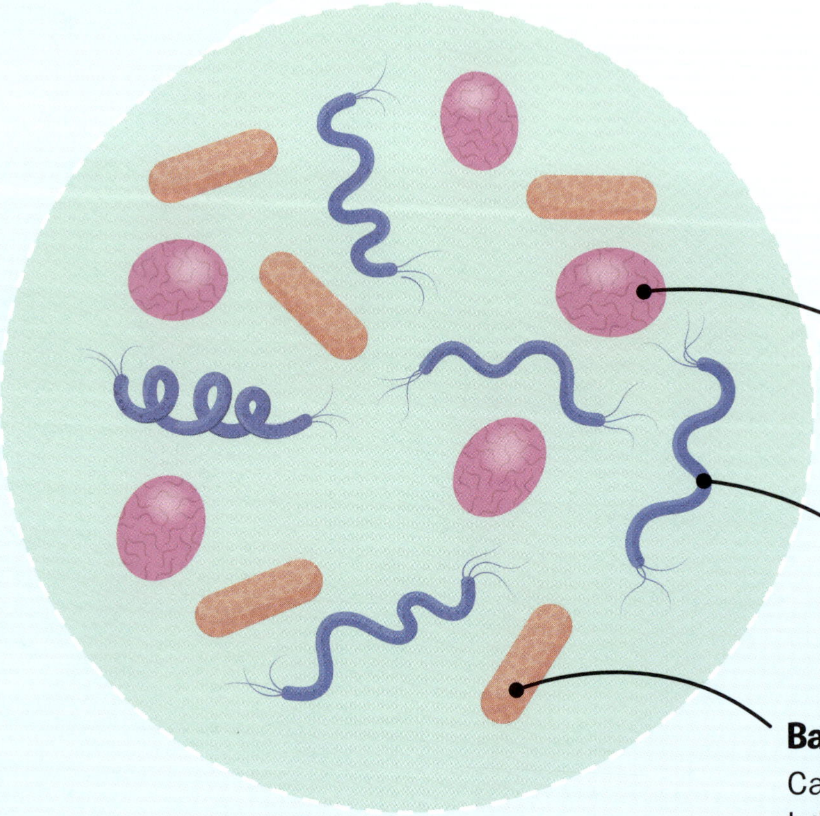

Cocci

Causes pneumonia, scarlet fever and meningitis.

Spirilla

Causes upset stomachs.

Bacilli

Causes tetanus, tuberculosis (TB), whooping cough and diphtheria.

What are viruses?

Viruses are so tiny you need high-powered microscopes to see them. They can't live by themselves, but invade cells in your body and take them over.

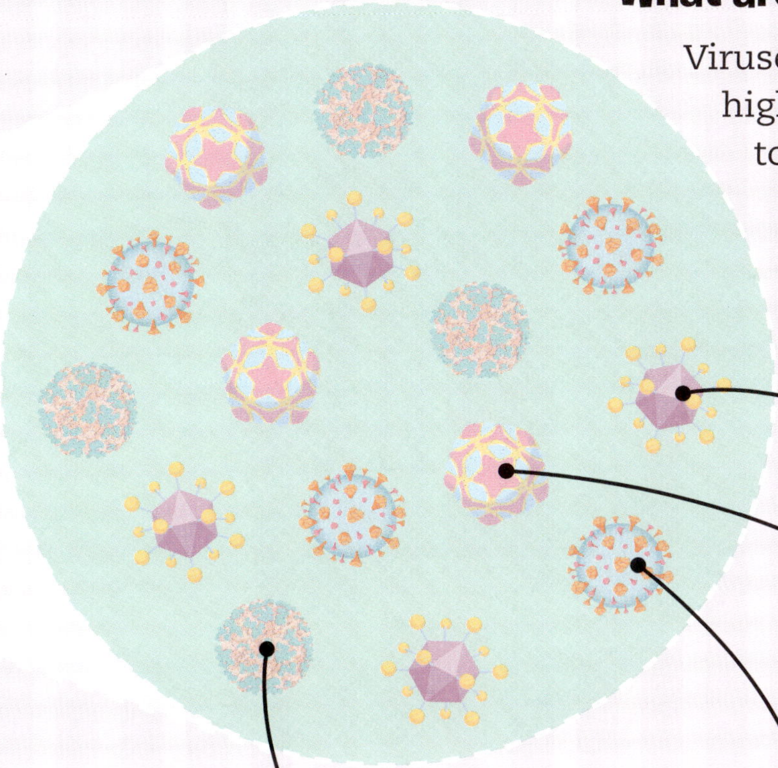

Adenoviruses
Causes conjunctivitis and upset stomachs.

Rhinovirus
Causes colds.

Coronavirus
Causes COVID-19.

Togavirus
Causes German measles.

Why do germs make me feel bad?

They can damage your body by releasing poisons or upsetting how your body works. But fever (hotness) and aches are signs that your body is fighting off the germs.

MUSCLES AND BONES
ON THE SURFACE
BRAIN, NERVES AND SENSES
HEARTBEATS, BLOOD AND BREATHING
FOOD, FARTS AND DIGESTION
KEEPING WELL

GERM BATTLES

When you get infected by germs, it can be bad. So how does your body fight back?

How do germs get in?

Your skin keeps most germs out, but they can get into your body through cuts, and through your eyes, nose and mouth.

What happens if germs get in?

You have an army of white blood cells to fight germs.

They can identify germs at once by their antigens, which act like ID tags, and go on the attack.

Some big white blood cells swallow germs whole!

MUSCLES AND BONES
ON THE SURFACE
BRAIN, NERVES AND SENSES
HEARTBEATS, BLOOD AND BREATHING
FOOD, FARTS AND DIGESTION
KEEPING WELL

GOT A CURE?

Viruses can cause your body a lot of problems, but luckily you have secret weapons to fight them, called antibodies.

What are antibodies?

Sneaky viruses hide away inside cells in your body, but they leave antigens on their surface.

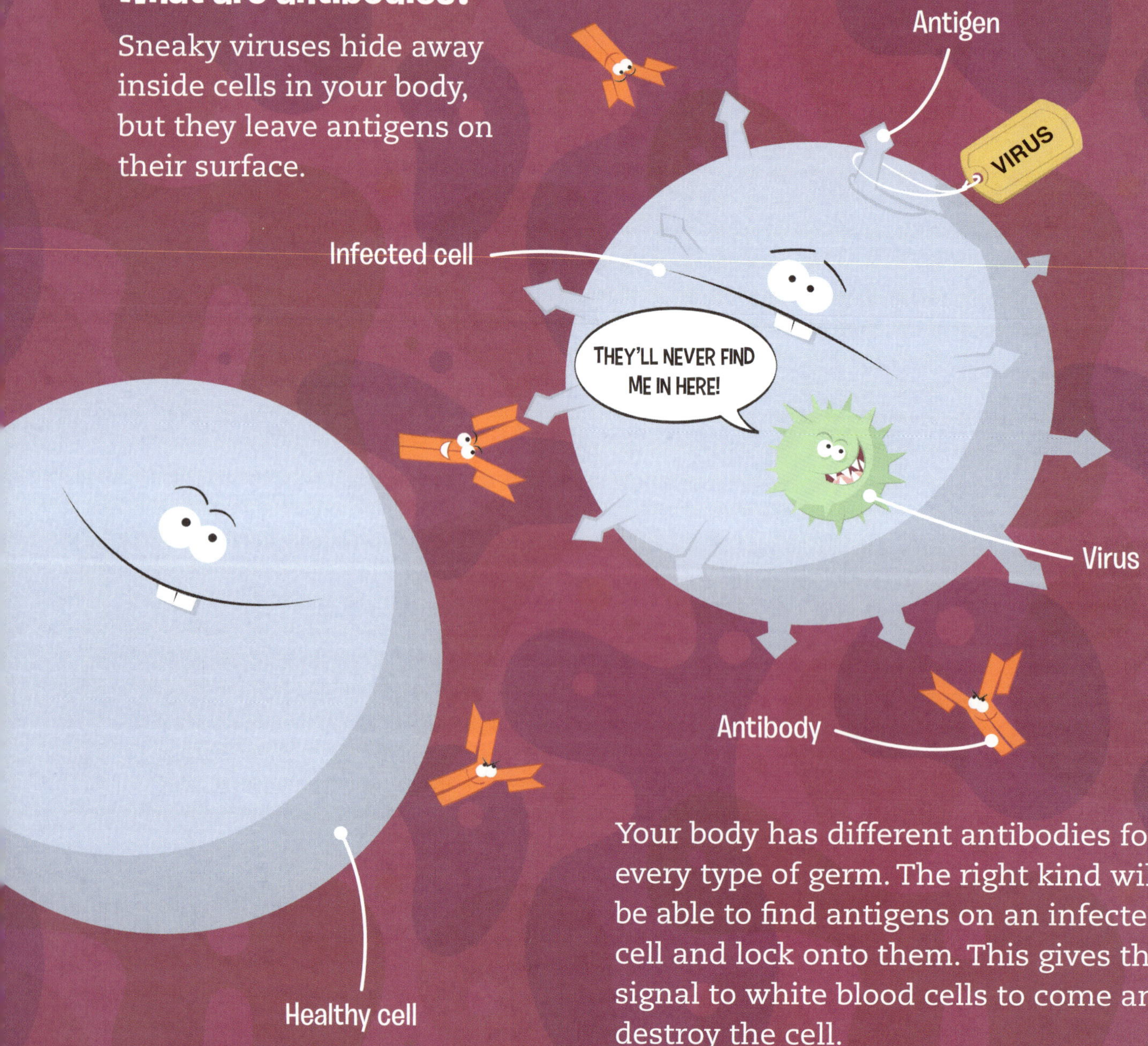

Your body has different antibodies for every type of germ. The right kind will be able to find antigens on an infected cell and lock onto them. This gives the signal to white blood cells to come and destroy the cell.

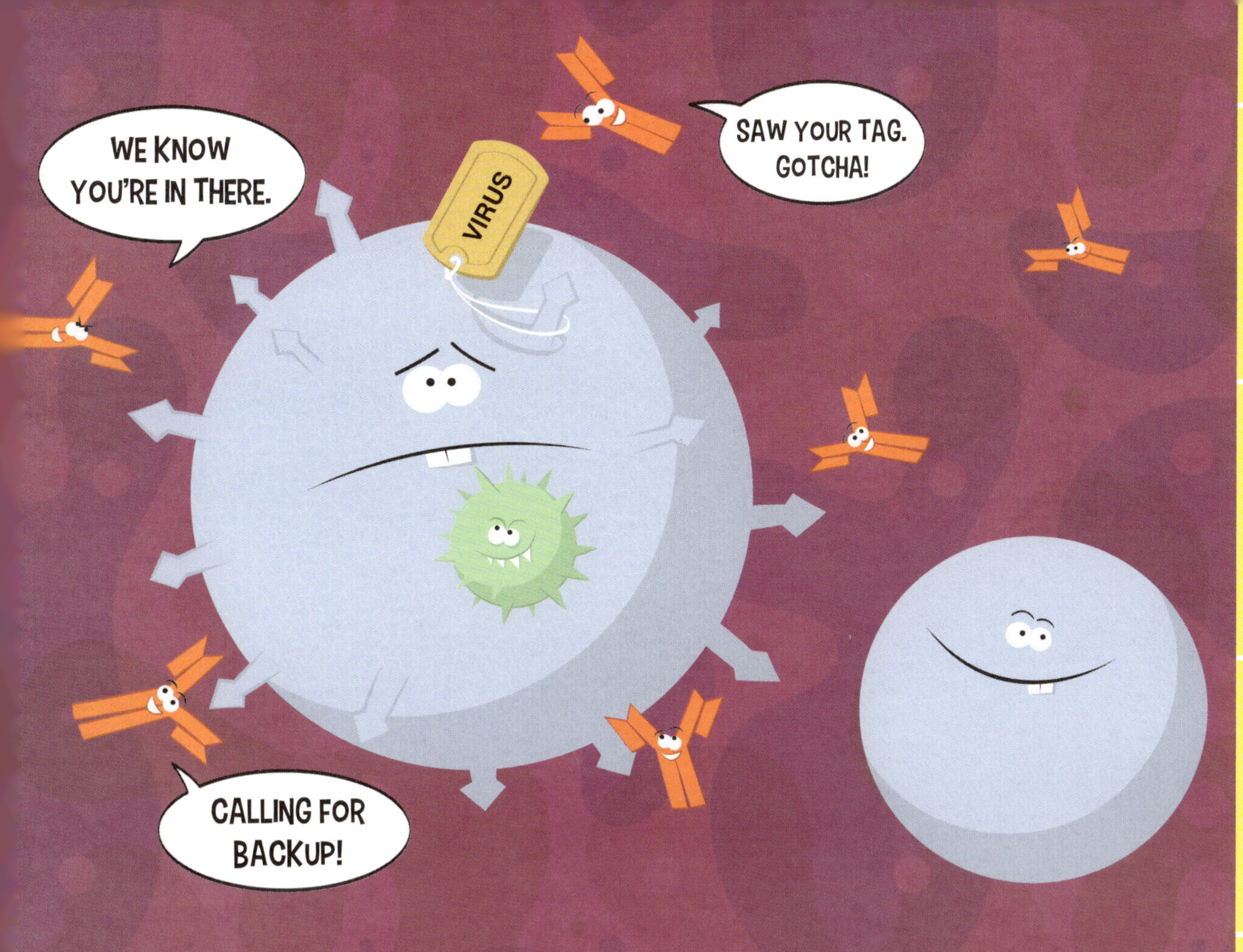

When germs are found, the right antibodies multiply like mad and hunt them down.

What is a vaccine?

Vaccines help stop you getting ill by giving you a harmless version of a germ. Your body reacts by building a store of antibodies, ready to fight off the real germ.

MUSCLES AND BONES
ON THE SURFACE
BRAIN, NERVES AND SENSES
HEARTBEATS, BLOOD AND BREATHING
FOOD, FARTS AND DIGESTION
KEEPING WELL

SNOT AND SNEEZES

Let's get nosy and find out what's going on up your nose!

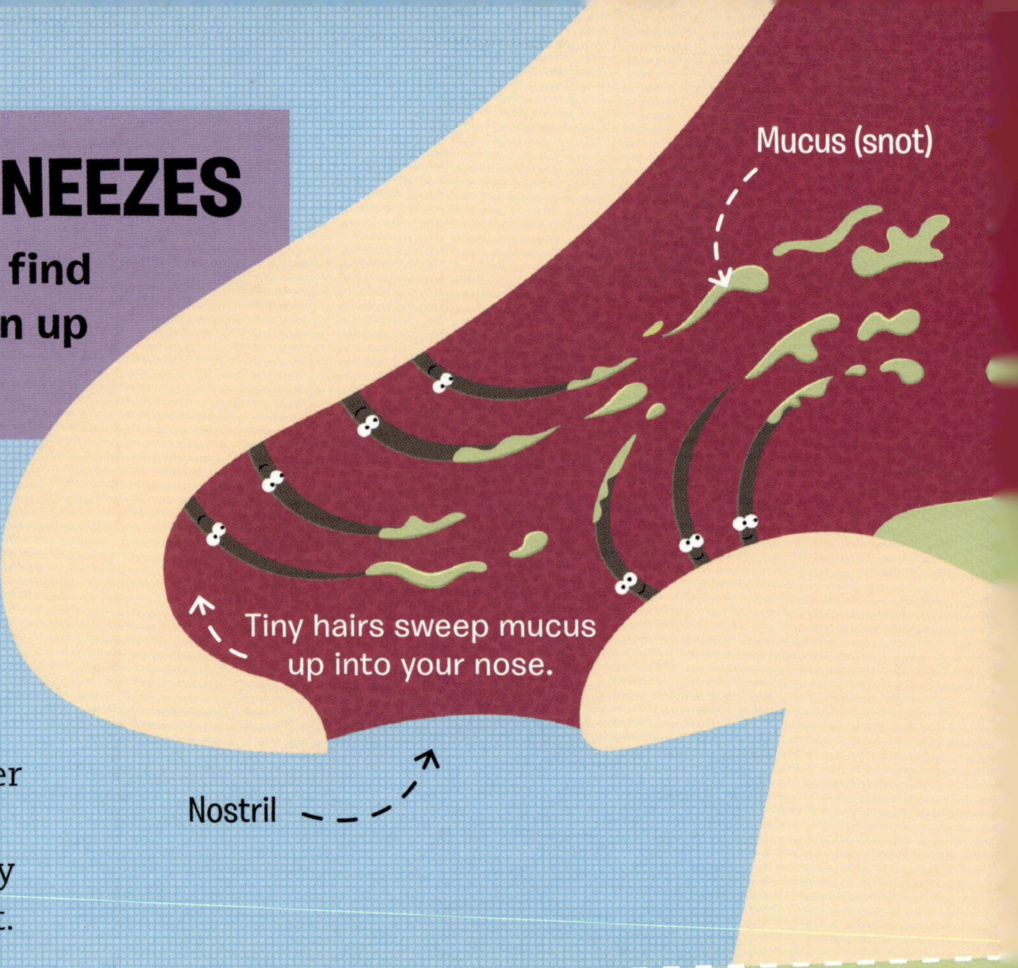

What is snot?

Snot is mostly water, with oils to make it thick and slimy, and some stuff that helps fight infection. Its proper name is mucus and it protects your airways by trapping germs and dirt.

Why does my nose run?

If you have a cold, your nose goes into snot overdrive to keep out germs. It can react the same way to things you are allergic to, such as pollen, thinking they are germs.

Cold weather can make your nose run, too!

Snot gets filled with junk that you breathe in, such as dust, pollen, germs, sand, smoke and particles from outer space!

Why do we sneeze?

It's your nose and airways' way of rebooting, like when you restart a computer. Sneezing clears out all the mucky mess so that you can start fresh.

How many times can you sneeze?

The world record for sneezing is held by a girl named Donna Griffiths, who sneezed one million times in a row, for two and a half years, between 1981 and 1983!

GLOSSARY

airways
The tubes that run from your nose and mouth to your lungs, which you breathe through. The tiny tubes inside your lungs are also called airways.

bacteria
Tiny living things made from just one cell.

cartilage
A tough, rubbery material. It makes your nose and ears bendy, and acts like a cushion in your knees.

digestion
The process of breaking down food in your body.

enamel (tooth)
A hard, smooth substance that covers and protects your teeth.

germs
Tiny living things, including bacteria and viruses, that can make you ill if they get inside your body.

infections
When germs invade your body and cause it harm.

microbes
Tiny living things, such as germs, which are too small to see without using a microscope.

milliseconds
There are 1,000 milliseconds in a second.

oxygen
A gas found in the air that most living things need to live.

pus
a thick, yellowish-white fluid that can form in response to an infection (*see infections*).

scalp
The skin on your head, under your hair.

senses
Nerve endings that detect changes in the world around you or inside your body, including heat and light.

sensors
Something that picks up on certain physical things from the world around you, such as heat, light, sound, taste and smell.

toxins
Poisonous substances created by living things.

vibrating
Shaking, or moving back and forth (or up and down) very quickly.